100%
AMERICAN

DANIEL EVAN WEISS

Illustrated by Patrick McDonnell

POSEIDON PRESS

NEW YORK LONDON TORONTO SYDNEY TOKYO

Poseidon Press
Simon & Schuster Building
Rockefeller Center
1230 Avenue of the Americas
New York, New York 10020

POSEIDON PRESS is a registered trademark
of Simon & Schuster Inc.

POSEIDON PRESS colophon is a trademark
of Simon & Schuster Inc.

Designed by Karolina Harris
Manufactured in the United States of America

1   3   5   7   9   10   8   6   4   2

Library of Congress Cataloging in Publication Data
Weiss, Daniel Evan.
100% American / Daniel Evan Weiss; illustrated by Patrick
McDonnell.
p.   cm.
1. United States—Miscellanea—Statistics.   I. Title.   II. Title:
One hundred percent American.
E156.W45 1988
973—dc19   88-18753
                                          CIP

ISBN 0-671-66872-2

Acknowledgments

Kind thanks to:
Wayne Parsons of Kane, Parsons, and Associates, Inc.;
Kathy Rich and Allan Kalish of *Seventeen* Magazine; Michael Bucuvalas and John Boyle of Schulman, Ronca, & Bucuvalas, Inc.; Jill Hodges of Louis Harris and Associates, Inc.; Ingrid Groller of *Parents* Magazine; Mary Hama of the Human Nutrition Information Service of the US Department of Agriculture; Nicholas Iadicicco of Opinion Research Corporation; Jeffrey Harris of RH Bruskin Associates Market Research; Jonathan Seder for his computer virtuosity; and, of course, Ann Patty.

For Gram,
Mom,
Dad,
and Judy,
born 100% American,
and Sid,
bred 100% American

Preface

I've watched the Bicentennial and the Statue of Liberty celebrations, as well as every Super Bowl, on TV. I like beer and hot dogs, trucks, and women in heels. If someone had asked I would have sworn that I was all-American. And I was. But I had never bothered to consider just what that meant.

Then, one Sunday in the bleachers, I found myself caught between two groups of fellows more interested in bluntly doubting each other's citizenship credentials and residency status than in the events on the field. I had never heard Americanism used this way. And it seemed all the odder here among the plenty—baseball, beer, hot dogs, even a few women in heels.

My complacency about my country, given this gentle nudge, was suddenly gone. I began examining everything I had always taken for granted, desperate to identify the national character. I soon understood that it could not be readily grasped, that it was not a quality or characteristic we all share. It was piecework. So I set about, like Betsy Ross with a quilt, to stitch together, one block at a time, this book, my American portrait. My fabric is statistics, drawn from the work of many keen observers of the national condition; the sources are listed in the appendix and numbered and keyed to the entries throughout the book.

Now when I watch TV, drinking a beer, eating a hot dog, admiring women in heels, I have a scientific appreciation of what it is to be American.

100% American

1%

1% of Americans read the Bible more than once a day. 110

1% of Americans do not believe in God. 119

1% of Americans don't know if they have a firearm in their home. 210

1% of American beer drinkers drinkers drink at least a six-pack per sitting. 288

1% of Americans are under legal probation. 112

1% of American households are not heated. 136

1% of American babies do not live one year. 102

1% of American adults speak Italian at home. 118

1% of Americans think the most important problem facing their community is indifference. 210

1% of American cat litter boxes are found in the living room. 116

1% of American chefs and restaurant owners think Minneapolis is the gastronomic capital of America. 127

1% of American teenage girls who send Mother's Day cards send six or more a year. 167

1% of American parents say their children don't watch enough TV. 108

1% of Americans are color-blind. 134

1% of American rape victims use or brandish a gun or knife at their attacker. 194

1% of American veterans aged 55 and older who do not use Veterans Administration hospitals do not because they think the hospitals experiment on people needlessly. 211

1% of American marines and sailors desert. 112

1% of American robberies are committed in a bank. 210

1% of American corporate profits are given as philanthropy.

1% of Americans say Tuesday is their favorite day of the week. 117

1% of Americans feel happiest in February. 252

1% of American income tax returns are examined by the IRS. 112

1% of Americans think hanging is the most humane form of capital punishment. 171

1% of Americans on Death Row are under 20 years of age. 112

1% of Americans play the accordion. 117

1% of Americans who murder law enforcement officers die in custody. 210

1% of American butter eaters consume at least 11 pats a sitting. 288

1% of American pancake eaters eat more than 16 a sitting. 288

1% of American leading scientists think there is a reasonable chance that lower back pain will be eliminated by the year 2000. 218

1% of Americans, if in search of the spiciest experience could spend a day with anyone in the world, would choose Pope John Paul. 128

1% of Americans would not like Catholics as neighbors. 152

2%

2% of America is owned by Indians. 112

2% of Americans go to a bar or tavern almost every day. 119

2% of Americans die in automobile accidents. 112

2% of American chief executives of large companies think the stock of their company is overvalued. 243

2% of Americans have ulcers. 134

2% of American households have a hamster, guinea pig, gerbil, mouse, or rat. 116

2% of Americans think the federal income tax they pay is too low. 153

2% of American law enforcement officers who are killed are slain by someone mentally deranged. 210

2% of American marriages are interracial. 112

2% of American murders are committed by strangulation. 101

2% of Americans have frequent constipation. 134

2% of Americans never socialize with close friends, relatives, or neighbors. 267

2% of American wives always initiate sex. 115

2% of Americans are at their best after midnight. 117

2% of Americans 12 years old and younger are arrested. 210

2% of American births are twins. 221

2% of Americans think the ideal number of children in a family is zero. 110 lol

2% of Americans live on farms. 112

2% of Americans think the government should own the automobile industry. 119

2% of Americans think communism is a good form of government. 119

2% of Americans never pray. 119

2% of Americans who suffer from premenstrual or menstrual pain consult a spiritual counselor or faith healer about their pain. 267

2% of Americans are cocaine users. 102

2% of American deaths are suicides. 102

2% of American leading scientists think there is a reasonable chance that cancer will be eliminated by the year 2000. 218

2% of American endangered species are snails. 112

2% of American high school seniors have set fire to someone's property on purpose in the last year. 210

2% of Americans would not like Protestants as neighbors. 152

2% of Americans think Jacqueline Onassis was history's most exciting figure. 128

2% of American wives who use devices for sexual stimulation during lovemaking use feathers. 115

3%

3% of American women of child-bearing age use the withdrawal method of contraception. 229

3% of Americans think the word *risk* usually describes something good. 231

3% of American 16-year-old girls give birth. 102

3% of Americans think George Washington was history's most exciting figure. 128

3% of American chefs and restaurant owners think Americanizing food means making it of poor quality. 127

3% of Americans eat dinner at work. 120

3% of American convicted burglars are sentenced to life in prison or death. 194

3% of Americans think the courts deal too harshly with criminals. 150

3% of American entertainment celebrities care most, among all national issues, about animal rights. 130

3% of Americans 25 years old and older have four or fewer years of education. 112

3% of American teenage girls who send Valentine's Day cards send 25 or more a year. 167

3% of American marines and sailors go AWOL. 112

3% of American television news anchors, if not in television, would be airline pilots. 126

3% of American robberies occur in gas stations. 101

3% of American teenage girls think quality is an unimportant factor when they buy shoes. 179

3% of American garbage is rubber and leather. 112

3% of Americans aged 8 to 17 think their family spends too much time together. 246

3% of Americans have migraines. 112

3% of Americans live in states with populations under one million. 112

3% of Americans never eat candy. 191

3% of American wives find fellatio repulsive. 115

3% of Americans think Cleopatra was history's most exciting figure. 128

3% of Americans think a firing squad is the most humane form of capital punishment. 171

3% of Americans think the development of the telephone has made life worse. 113

3% of Americans who earn the minimum wage or less work for the Federal Government. 186

3% of Americans who murder law enforcement officers then kill themselves. 210

3% of Americans would not like Jews as neighbors. 152

3% of American wives need more than 25 minutes of intercourse before they reach orgasm. 115

3% of Americans think dancing is the best way to spend an evening. 110

3% of Americans think Elvis Presley was history's most exciting figure. 128

4%

4% of American women do not own panties. 125

4% of Americans haven't seen a doctor in at least five years. 134

4% of American households contain six people or more. 112

4% of American cheese is Swiss cheese. 112

4% of American garbage is wood. 112

4% of American girls began menstruating at age 15 or older. 161

4% of American immigrants come from India. 112

4% of American mothers do not think it is too important to use strict discipline with children. 212

4% of American lawyers think the Constitution is out of date. 139

4% of American teenage girls feel their parents are not strict enough. 192

4% of American teenage girls would not vote for a qualified woman for president. 192

4% of American women executives prefer a female boss. 117

4% of American women do not own a bra. 125

4% of American rapes not reported to the police were considered too unimportant by the victim. 194

4% of American wives who have had more than 10 extramarital lovers say their marriage is very good. 115

4% of American wives never initiate sex. 115

4% of American men weigh 230 pounds or more. 280

4% of Americans aged 65 or older are divorced. 196

4% of American teenage girls do not plan to marry. 192

4% of Americans have asthma. 134

4% of Americans think solar energy will worsen the quality of life for people like themselves. 245

4% of American high school seniors have used crack in the last year. 206

4% of American high school seniors have used LSD in the last year. 210

4% of Americans think the country is spending too much money dealing with drug addiction. 150

5%

5% of American women who have become more cautious about sex from fear of AIDS no longer practice oral sex. 229

5% of Americans have hemorrhoids. 112

5% of American law enforcement officers who are killed are slain in family quarrels. 210

5% of American girls began to date at age 12 or younger. 192

5% of Americans first learned about sex from their father. 116

5% of American chefs and restaurant owners eat in their own restaurants but do not eat what the customers eat. 127

5% of Americans go to McDonald's each day. 187

5% of American high school seniors have shoplifted five or more times in the last year. 210

5% of American high school seniors drink every day. 206

5% of American violent crime occurs in school. 194

5% of Americans think there is not enough emphasis on football in most high schools. 165

5% of American women corporate officers disagree with the women's movement. 149

5% of American women corporate officers wouldn't be caught dead in the kitchen. 149

5% of American chocolate-chip-cookie-eaters eat more than eight at a sitting. 288

5% of American fishers, hunters, and trappers are women. 112

5% of American women of child-bearing age are trying to conceive. 229

5% of American cat litter boxes are found in the bedroom. 116

5% of American women of child-bearing age do not have sex. 229

5% of Americans have had headaches on more than 100 days in the last year. 267

5% of Americans are mostly or very dissatisfied with their family life. 110

5% of Americans have, or know someone personally close to them who has, been involved in an airplane accident. 231

5% of Americans think John. F. Kennedy was history's most exciting figure. 128

5% of American blacks would like to live in a neighborhood that is mostly white. 119

5% of Americans are afraid of being alone in a house at night. 113

5% of Americans live in mobile homes. 117

5% of Americans smoke in bed on a regular basis. 231

5% of American teenage girls aspire to be a secretary or clerical worker. 192

5% of American teenage girls aspire to be an actress, dancer, or in show business. 192

5% of American teenage girls who use cosmetic bleach put it on their stomach. 161

5% of Americans think only men should be gynecologists. 244

5% of Americans think Jesus Christ was history's most exciting figure. 128

5% of American households do not purchase bread. 284

5% of Americans expect the afterlife to be boring. 269

6%

6% of Americans aged 8 to 17 say their home life would be better if their parents treated them less as an adult. 246

6% of American girls began menstruating at age 10 or younger. 161

6% of American brides are first married under the age of 18. 200

6% of American unmarried couples who live together are aged 65 and older. 112

6% of American children under 18 years of age have mothers who never married. 112

6% of Americans with children in the home do not think the children inherited their parents' good looks. 283

6% of Americans feel the single greatest element in happiness is great wealth. 252

6% of American cat litter boxes are found in the kitchen. 116

6% of American crimes of violence occur inside a restaurant or bar. 210

6% of Americans have drunk wine in the last 24 hours. 153

6% of American women sleep in the nude. 117

6% of Americans are foreign-born. 118

6% of American television news anchors, if not in television, would be actors. 126

6% of Americans find life dull. 117

6% of Americans have been to the dentist at least five times in the last year. 134

6% of American workers say their boss's decision-making style is do-nothing. 232

6% of Americans prefer not to work around people who are physically disabled. 152

6% of American workers walk to work. 118

6% of American males think community standards regulating sexually explicit material should be less strict. 210

6% of American men who are murdered are done in by wives or girlfriends. 101

6% of American murders are committed with blunt objects. 101

6% of American murders are committed without a weapon. 194

6% of American prison inmates got no further in school than kindergarten. 194

6% of Americans think the country spends too much on education. 150

6% of Americans think teachers should not be required to pass a competency test before being hired. 165

6% of American large-size women have trouble finding girdles of suitable size and style. 124

6% of American deaths are caused by accidents. 102

7%

7% of American adults drink half of the alcohol consumed in America. 206

7% of American teenage girls have had violence done to them by a date. 192

7% of American blacks approve of the South African system of apartheid. 168

7% of American casino game winnings are made at the roulette wheel. 205

7% of Americans think gambling is not risky. 231

7% *of American high school seniors have taken a part of a car without the permission of the owner in the last year.* 210

7% of Americans say "mood" is their favorite type of music. 236

7% of American garbage is plastics. 112

7% of Americans water ski. 112

7% of American teenage girls own golf clubs. 204

7% of American physicians do not very much trust current scientific knowledge about AIDS transmission. 174

7% of American women of child-bearing age use the diaphragm or sponge for contraception. 229

7% of American women aged 15 to 44 give birth each year. 102

7% of American households do not purchase eggs. 284

7% of American newborns weigh less than 5½ pounds. 178

7% of American immigrants come from China. 112

7% of Americans would be troubled if astronomers discovered that the universe is constant in size. 254

7% of Americans are victims of crimes of theft each year. 210

7% of Americans think the amount of money awarded to patients by juries in malpractice suits is usually not enough. 131

7% of American wives never attain orgasm during intercourse. 115

7% of Americans have varicose veins of their lower extremities. 112

7% of American women are less concerned now than a year ago about personal appearance. 229

7% of Americans think God is more like a mother figure than a father figure. 116

7% of Americans think Jews have too much power in America. 152

7% of Americans think a person has a right to commit suicide if he has dishonored his family. 119

7% of Americans think a person has a right to commit suicide if he has gone bankrupt. 119

8%

8% of American wives have sexual intercourse twenty or more times a month. 115

8% of American women who eat candy do so every day. 191

8% of American women corporate officers think being a woman has made success easier to attain. 149

8% of Americans think the American steel industry has declined because of federal regulations. 201

8% of American full-time workers are hurt on the job each year. 102

8% of American adults play racquet ball. 112

8% of American high school seniors could have five drinks and then drive a car, and they think their close friends would not disapprove. 153

8% of Americans, if they had the ability, would love making an Evil Knievel-type jump on a motorcycle. 128

8% of American teenage girls own a motor scooter. 204

8% of American high school students go to private schools. 112

8% of Americans have a heart condition. 112

8% of Americans say they suffer great stress almost every day. 267

8% of American physicians believe too much money is being spent on AIDS research. 174

8% of American teenage girls are not concerned about the death of a parent. 192

8% of Americans aged 18 to 24 carry a hidden weapon. 210

8% of American thefts of less than $10 are reported to the police. 194

8% of Americans use marijuana. 102

8% of American cocaine users have taken it intravenously. 251

8% of Americans are heavy drinkers. 102

8% of Americans 18 years old and older are divorced. 112

8% of Americans 18 years old and older are widowed. 112

8% of American teenage girls do not plan to have children. 192

8% of American 17-year-olds think Abraham Lincoln wrote *Uncle Tom's Cabin.* 207

8% of Americans would object strongly if a family member wanted to bring a black friend home to dinner. 119

8% of Americans receive food stamps. 112

9%

9% of American adults roller skate. 112

9% of Americans say they don't watch enough TV. 108

9% of Americans have had backaches on more than 100 days in the last year. 267

9% of American adults sleep nine or more hours a night. 116

9% of American chefs and restaurant owners do not eat in their own restaurants. 127

9% of American exports are food, drink, and tobacco. 208

9% of American forest fires in protected areas are caused by lightning. 112

9% of American teenage girls have curly hair. 162

9% of American wives masturbate because their husbands enjoy watching. 115

9% of Americans think organ transplants will worsen the quality of life for people like themselves. 245

9% of Americans aged 12 to 17 have experimented with inhalants. 206

9% of Americans often have a *déjà vu*. 119

9% of Americans think almost all people running local government are dishonest or crooked. 110

9% of Americans think Jimmy Carter was one of America's three greatest presidents. 111

9% of American women would like to change their ears. 116

9% of Americans think the gas chamber is the most humane form of capital punishment. 171

9% of Americans prefer not to work around people who have cancer. 152

9% of American lawyers feel AIDS victims can lawfully be evicted from their apartments. 144

9% of Americans would not like Hispanics as neighbors. 152

9% of American wives never perform fellatio on their husbands. 115

9% of Americans think the Catholic Church has too much power in America. 152

9% of American women aged 15 to 19 are engaged to their partner when they first have intercourse. 277

9% of American men aged 17 to 21 have just recently met their partner when they first have intercourse. 277

10%

10% of American hairdressers and cosmetologists are men. 112

10% of American truck drivers are women. 112

10% of American men feel that marriage costs them their individual identity. 223

10% of American babies are unwanted at the time of conception. 112

10% *of American teenage girls think people in need should not be helped, as they probably brought it on themselves.* 202

10% of American women personally know someone who has AIDS. 229

10% of Americans are allergic to ragweed. 182

10% of American chefs and restaurant owners think American food is a fad that will not last long. 127

10% of Americans think black and white students should go to separate schools. 119

10% of Americans think college athletes should have to maintain a higher academic standard than other students because they get a free education. 165

10% of Americans are members of a health club or fitness center. 110

10% of Americans use tents or RVs for accommodations during their summer vacation. 213

10% of Americans say the automobile is the greatest invention of all time. 117

10% of Americans who do not always wear seatbelts do not because their car, life, and health are fully insured. 231

10% of Americans say religion in the home hasn't strengthened family relations at all. 110

10% of Americans read the Bible daily. 110

10% of Americans are perfectly comfortable if their home is not neat and clean. 252

10% of American shoppers think in-store music would enhance their experience in a supermarket. 257

10% of Americans think of God as a liberator. 116

10% of Americans think the universe is getting smaller. 254

11%

11% of Americans favor co-ed high school wrestling teams. 110

11% of American women are less than five feet tall. 279

11% of American women earn the minimum wage or less. 186

11% of American men think women should pay their equal share of all expenses on dates. 223

11% of Americans are not sure if the Soviet Union is friendly or hostile toward America. 238

11% of American children in one-parent households live with their fathers. 185

11% of American adults buy take-out food each day. 116

11% of American parents of students under 18 never enforce study hours. 212

11% of American crimes are committed by youngsters under 15 years of age. 101

11% of Americans have hardly any confidence in the US Supreme Court. 151

11% of Americans think that America has never used nuclear weapons in a war. 117

11% of American teenage girls use breath spray. 161

11% of American women think it is acceptable to have extramarital sex. 229

11% of American women who have become more cautious about sex from fear of AIDS are celibate. 229

11% of American married men think women attach too much importance to sex and should treat it more casually. 223

11% of Americans expect to see total peace between nations in their lifetime. 252

11% of American companies have a foreigner on their board of directors. 215

11% of Americans speak a language other than English at home. 117

11% of Americans think blacks have too much power in America. 152

11% of American general aviation accidents involve alcohol. 250

11% of American wives attain orgasm during intercourse once in a while. 115

11% of Americans killed in motor vehicle accidents were riding motorcycles. 112

11% of American women do not think marriage is a commitment for life. 229

11% of Americans aged 18 to 25 do not really think their greatest achievements are still ahead of them. 252

11% of American teenage girls who play board games don't enjoy them too much. 177

11% of Americans claim to know a great deal about the gallbladder. 253

12%

12% of American 17-year-olds think the First World War was fought before 1800. [207]

12% of Americans seldom or never read a newspaper. [252]

12% of Americans drink five or more cups of coffee a day. [120]

12% of Americans have high blood pressure. [134]

12% of American adults have 17 or more dental fillings. [163]

12% of American chefs and restaurant owners think Americanizing food means making it bland or plain. 127

12% of American mothers gain less than 16 pounds during pregnancy. 178

12% of Americans go birdwatching or study nature. 112

12% of American households have both a cat and a dog. 116

12% of Americans say classical is their favorite type of music. 236

12% of American law enforcement officers who are killed were off-duty. 210

12% of Americans aged 30 to 34 are arrested. 210

12% of American motor vehicle thefts not reported to the police are not reported because the victim thinks it is a private matter. 194

12% of American teenagers lost their virginity in a car. 117

12% of American grocery stores sell male contraceptives. 247

12% of American teenage girls use a douche. 161

12% of American high school seniors go out with a date more than three times a week. 153

12% of Americans would be unwilling to increase their taxes for programs tracing missing children. 212

12% of Americans with children under 18 are pessimistic about their children's future. 212

12% of American television news anchors would rather dine alone than with the current president or any living ex-president. 126

12% of American men drink alcohol every day. 210

12% of Americans are 65 years old or older. 112

12% of Americans over the age of 65 live in poverty. 150

12% of Americans gamble on a regular basis. 231

12% of American households pay their bills exclusively in cash. 117

12% of Americans who are married feel single adults are more contented than married ones. 252

12% of Americans would not like unmarried couples as neighbors. 152

12% of Americans prefer Chinese food when they eat out. 116

12% of Americans think Asians have too much power in America. 152

12% of Americans, even given the time and money, would have little or no interest in going around the world in 80 days. 128

13%

13% of American babies are born to teenage mothers. 112

13% of American wives first had sex when they were no more than 15 years old. 115

13% of Americans use condoms or plan to start soon. 286

13% of American women veterans of World War II began their active service at age 30 or older. 226

13% of American parents say they are stricter than their own parents were. 106

13% of American married women have become more cautious about sex because of fear of AIDS. 229

13% of American endangered species are clams. 112

13% of American grocery stores have a salad bar. 247

13% of American high school seniors have used cocaine in the last year. 210

13% of Americans aged 16 to 18 are arrested. 210

13% of American teenage girls who use mouthwash use it less than once a week. 161

13% of American high school seniors never go out with a date. 153

13% of American women consider themselves pretty. 117

13% of American women aged 21 to 35 think that if a woman combines a career with homemaking her husband might have less respect for her. 122

13% of American commercial airline accidents are caused by the aircraft or its engines. 217

13% of Americans have arthritis. 112

13% of Americans claim to know a great deal about the intestines. 253

13% of Americans are enrolled in Medicare. 102

13% of Americans who were hospitalized in the last year were discharged before they felt well enough to leave. *174*

13% of Americans jog. 110

13% of Americans would not like blacks as neighbors. 152

13% of Americans would not like religious fundamentalists as neighbors. 152

13% of American violent crime occurs in or around the victim's home. 194

13% of Americans think a person has a right to commit suicide if he is tired of living and ready to die. 119

13% of American whites have tried a hallucinogen. 251

13% of Americans aged 13 to 17 believe in the Loch Ness Monster. 268

14%

14% of Americans snack all day. 120

14% of Americans live below the poverty line. 112

14% of American adults hunt. 112

14% of American dollars gambled are played in slot machines. 205

14% of American teenage girls play *Wheel of Fortune.* 177

14% of Americans killed in motor vehicle accidents were pedestrians. 112

14% of American families own a business. 112

14% of American workers say their boss's decision-making style is wavering. 232

14% of American high school seniors have damaged school property on purpose in the last year. 210

14% of American married women say they have been raped by their husbands. 117

14% of American men are less then 5'6" tall. 280

14% of American physicians feel that children with AIDS should not be allowed to attend regular school classes. 174

14% of Americans have checked their horoscope in the last 24 hours. 153

14% of Americans feel happiest in June. 252

14% of Americans feel happiest in December. 252

14% of American suicides hang or strangle themselves. 112

14% of Americans who die are cremated. 148

14% of Americans think communism is OK for some countries. 150

14% of Americans have used a credit card in the last 24 hours. 153

14% of Americans think science and technology have done the human race more harm than good. 113

14% of Americans think that if someone had a genetic defect fatal both to the patient and to children who inherited it, doctors should be allowed to correct the gene affecting future generations, but not the one afflicting the patient. 245

15%

15% of American 17-year-olds believe the Spanish knight who attacked windmills thinking they were giants was Zorro. 207

15% of American high school seniors have had trouble getting started at least 20 of the last 30 mornings. 271

15% of American women think a happy marriage is possible without children. 193

15% of American women veterans were forced by the military to leave because of a pregnancy or children. 226

15% of Americans think that government is both the problem and the answer. 150

15% of American women think it would be acceptable for their single daughters to have and raise a child. 193

15% of American married men say they do most of the cooking in the household. 272

15% of American men feel their family causes them a lot of stress. 223

15% of American college students spend more than half their waking hours worrying. 117

15% of American teenage girls own at least ten fragrances. 170

15% of Americans have chronic sinusitis. 134

15% of Americans who oppose the death penalty for convicted murderers think the punishment should be left to God. 210

15% of Americans aged 13 to 17 believe in ghosts. 268

15% of American wives always attain orgasm during intercourse. 115

15% of American adults play basketball. 112

15% of Americans say their present life-style is full of spice, challenges, and excitement. 128

15% of American Indians die in alcohol-related accidents. 250

15% of American leading medical experts think an effective cure for AIDS will never be found. 218

16%

16% of Americans think that America should not militarily defend one of our major European allies if it is attacked by the Soviet Union. 189

16% of Americans aged 18 to 44 think America was right to fight the Vietnam War. 222

16% of Americans think that if the military draft were reinstated, homosexuals should be exempted. 119

16% of American women veterans are housewives. 226

16% of American wives often masturbate. 115

16% of American married men are sometimes confused about what women want sexually. 223

16% of American women aged 19 to 39 are always on a diet. 111

16% of Americans snack before bed. 120

16% of Americans often eat bananas. 287

16% of Americans think of the lungs as part of the digestive system. 253

16% of American men weigh 200 pounds or more. 280

16% of Americans like to be the center of attention. 252

16% of Americans have been affected, or know someone close to them who has been affected, by earthquakes. 231

16% of Americans are bothered quite a bit by getting older. 252

16% of American men aged 65 or older are in the labor force. 196

16% of American leading scientists think the limit to the human life span is over 115 years. 218

16% of Americans think the world is filled with evil and sin. 164

16% of America is Alaska. 112

16% of Americans who have not installed smoke detectors have not because they don't own their own home. 231

16% of Americans think that as a society we spend too much effort on women. 212

16% of Americans think America is spending too much money improving the conditions of blacks. 119

16% of American school superintendents favor busing of children to achieve racial balance. 199

16% of American private school teachers are uncertified. 112

16% of American commercial airline accidents are caused by traffic control. 217

16% of Americans think America should pull out of the United Nations. 119

16% of Americans aged 13 to 17 believe in Bigfoot. 268

17%

17% of American married women are more concerned now than a year ago about sexual satisfaction. 229

17% of American single women are less concerned now than a year ago about sexual satisfaction. 229

17% of Americans see God as a lover. 116

17% of Americans claim to know a great deal about hemorrhoids. 253

17% of Americans who are regular smokers have not quit because they take good care of themselves so they think it shouldn't hurt them. 231

17% of American physicians say all of their patients want a candid assessment of their medical condition, even if it is unfavorable. 227

17% of American doctors smoke. 117

17% of American homicides are committed by a relative of the victim. 194

17% of American teenage girls use an electric razor. 161

17% of Americans play tennis. 112

17% of American babies often eat chicken. 287

17% of American illegal gambling is on the numbers. 205

17% of Americans with children in the home do not hope the children will grow up and make a lot of money. 283

17% of Americans have had, or know someone personally close to them who has had, a personal financial crisis, such as being sued or going bankrupt. 231

17% of the beverages Americans drink is beer. 112

17% of Americans have drunk beer in the last 24 hours. 153

17% of American high school seniors favor a military draft. 271

17% of Americans favor a return of alcohol Prohibition. 210

17% of Americans feel there will be an atomic war in their lifetime. 252

18%

18% of American women would like to change the shape of their feet, for the most part to make them smaller. 116

18% of American high school seniors have gotten into a serious fight in school or at work in the last year. 210

18% of Americans aged 13 to 17 think schools should have the right to spank or physically discipline students. 246

18% of American women veteran officers were in or exposed to combat situations. 226

18% of American visitors from overseas come from Japan. 213

18% of American unmarried 15-year-old girls have had sexual intercourse. 112

18% of Americans aged 8 to 17 say their home life would be better if their parents were less involved with their personal life. 246

18% of American parents would be unwilling to serve as a Big Brother or Big Sister. 212

18% of American teenage girls who wear perfume began before age 12. 169

18% of American wives think the messiness after intercourse is the worst aspect of sex. 115

18% of American women of child-bearing age have had themselves sterilized for contraception. 229

18% of American workers live within 10 minutes of work. 118

18% of Americans aged 8 to 17 would grade their school cafeteria food an "F." 246

18% of Americans are underweight. 116

18% of Americans believe it's not wrong to cheat a little on taxes since the government spends too much money anyway. 114

18% of Americans aged 25 to 29 are arrested. 210

18% of Americans who do not always wear seatbelts do not because they are very careful drivers. 231

18% of Americans think the electric chair is the most humane form of capital punishment. 171

19%

19% of Americans would be troubled if astronomers discovered that the universe is expanding. 254

19% of American adults have a college degree. 150

19% of American 17-year-old students never read on their own. 207

19% of Americans aged 8 to 17 think most of their teachers expect too much from them. 246

19% of American girls aged 15 to 19 own a car. 204

19% of American households are heated by electricity. 136

19% of American reporters assigned to beats cover sports. 184

19% of American grocery stores sell footwear. 247

19% of American teenage girls use a depilatory. 161

19% of Americans aged 13 to 17 believe in witchcraft. 268

19% of American high school seniors are not eager to leave home and live independent of their parents. 271

19% of American men sleep in the nude. 117

19% of American men think a happy marriage is possible without children. 193

19% of American wives who vary locations to make sex more interesting choose the outdoors. 115

19% of American wives who have had extramarital affairs say their marriage is very good. 115

19% of American women aged 21 to 35 think a husband is unrelated to a fulfilling life. 122

19% of American women would like to have fewer muscles. 116

19% of American teenage girls use a feminine deodorant spray. 161

19% of American men would like to change their nose. 116

19% of Americans have eaten fish in the last 24 hours. 153

20%

20% of Americans would rather have a tooth pulled than take a car in for repairs. 117

20% of American workers get to work by carpool. 118

20% of American grocery stores sell female contraceptives. 247

20% of American suicides poison themselves. 112

20% of American babies often eat potatoes. 287

20% of American sixth-graders cannot locate the United States on a world map. 117

20% of American lawyers feel AIDS victims can lawfully be fired from their jobs. 144

20% of Americans think it is worse to let a guilty man go free than it is to convict an innocent one. 119

20% of American jail inmates have no legal counsel. 112

20% of Americans aged 25 to 74 have high blood pressure. 102

20% of American veterans aged 75 and older are not sure where they expect to be living ten years from now. 211

20% of Americans under the age of 18 live in poverty. 150

20% of Americans own stock. 225

20% of Americans have been affected, or know someone personally close to them who has been affected, by nuclear power plant accidents. 231.

20% of Americans say that if tests showed they were likely to get a serious or fatal genetic illness later in life, they would be unwilling to have those genes corrected. 245

20% of Americans over 65 years of age think arthritis and cancer are caused by vitamin or mineral deficiencies. 282

20% of Americans have had a doctor tell them to find another doctor if they disagree with the first doctor's diagnosis and recommendations for treatment. 227

20% of American rapes occur in the victim's home. 194

20% of American Indians die in accidents. 250

20% of Americans say that if they had their life to live over, they would not continue with their formal education. 252

20% of Americans are dissatisfied with their job or profession. 252

20% of American women have a bustline of more than 37 inches. 279

20% of American women have a bustline of less than 32 inches. 279

20% of Americans think it is not wise to plan ahead because many things turn out to be a matter of good or bad luck anyway. 270

21%

21% of American murders are committed with a knife. 210

21% of American robberies are committed with a knife. 194

21% of American babies are delivered by Caesarean section. 112

21% of Americans have refused to undergo treatment by a doctor. 227

21% of American adult patients are incapable of understanding their condition and treatment, according to their doctors. 227

21% of American lawyers are in solo practice. 143

21% of American adults camp. 112

21% of American wives think the best part of sex is satisfying their partner. 115

21% of Americans say people marry because marriage is better than living alone. 116

21% of American teenage girls do not think the ERA should be made law or a constitutional amendment. 192

21% of Americans have gotten up before 6 AM in the last 24 hours. 153

21% of America is cropland. 112

21% of Americans think the good person must avoid contamination by the corruption of the world. 164

21% of American women aged 21 to 35 think that a woman who never marries is not likely to find self-fulfillment. 122

21% of American babies are born to unmarried mothers. 102

21% of Americans first learned about sex from their mother. 116

21% of American guards are women. 112

21% of American women would like to change their nose. 116

21% of Americans think that America should not militarily defend Japan if it is attacked by the Soviet Union or China. 189

21% of American families own US savings bonds. 112

21% of American high school seniors think heroin is easy to come by. 210

21% of Americans think few if any teenagers can read and write adequately. 212

21% of American teenage girls think premarital sex is a bad idea for everyone. 192

22%

22% of Americans never read the Bible. 110

22% of American teenage girls are not concerned about nuclear war. 192

22% of Americans would be unwilling to increase their taxes for public schools. 212

22% of American women breast-feed their infants at 6 months of age. 102

22% of American potatoes are french-fried. 117

22% of American females aged 15 to 21 who own a car do the maintenance or repairs themselves. 181

22% of American men are shy about taking the sexual initiative. 223

22% of American new cases of syphilis are undiagnosed or untreated. 219

22% of American imports come from Japan. 208

22% of American workers are union members. 112

22% of Americans think the government should control wages. 119

22% of Americans aged 8 to 17 think their parents expect too much from them. 246

22% of Americans have read Ann Landers, Dear Abby, or a similar column in the last 24 hours. 153

22% of Americans 18 years old and older are single. 112

22% of Americans admitted to a state or county mental hospital have an alcohol-related disorder. 255

22% of Americans claim to know practically nothing at all about the liver. 253

22% of Americans die of cancer. 112

22% of Americans think homosexuals should not be hired as salespeople. 152

22% of Americans dislike opera. 236

22% of Americans who own homeowner's insurance are protected against earthquakes. 231

22% of Americans, if they had the time, money, and ability, would love to try climbing Mt. Everest. 128

23%

23% of American teenage girls were influenced by a boyfriend in their attitude about sex. 192

23% of Americans think most teenagers will have a teenage pregnancy. 212

23% of American men wonder whether they're as good a sexual partner as other men are. 223

23% of Americans feel surrogate motherhood should be illegal. 105

23% of Americans aged 50 and over think their greatest achievements are still ahead of them. 252

23% of Americans say they dream in black and white. 117

23% of Americans, if they had the ability, would love to try conducting the Chicago Symphony at Carnegie Hall. 128

23% of American 17-year-olds think that in Greek mythology Atlas had to map out the heavens. 207

23% of American teenage girls think that if there were a national draft, women should be drafted. 192

23% of Americans own a cat. 116

23% of Americans have been affected, or know someone personally close to them who has been affected, by forest fires. 231

23% of Americans who murder law enforcement officers are on parole or probation at the time. 210

23% of American murders have an unknown motive. 112

23% of Americans, even if there was no direct risk to humans, would disapprove of genetic manipulation to make more productive farm animals. 245

23% of American women weigh 160 pounds or more. 279

23% of American men weigh 150 pounds or less. 280

23% of Americans who have been punched or beaten have been punched or beaten both as a child and as an adult. 119

23% of Americans do not think they know how to take advantage of opportunities. 252

23% of Americans, if in search of the spiciest experience could spend a day with anyone in the world, would choose their own spouse. 128

24%

24% of American inmates of state prisons live in units with fifty or more inmates. 210

24% of American households contain only one person. 112

24% of American adults go to their in-laws for advice on important personal decisions. 104

24% of Americans aged 8 to 17 think their parents place too much emphasis on school grades. 246

24% of Americans have exercised in the last 24 hours. 153

24% of Americans always feel rushed to do things. 119

24% of American households grow fruits or berries. 112

24% of American households living above the poverty level receive Medicare. 112

24% of American high school seniors have been drivers in an automobile accident in the last year. 210

24% of Americans have had, or know someone personally close to them who has had, a fire in the home. 231

24% of Americans think stockholders are not much affected by what happens to a business. 230

24% of Americans think there should be laws forbidding marriages between blacks and whites. 119

24% of Americans who commit murder never appear in a courtroom. 117

24% of Americans with heart murmurs are under 18 years old. 134

24% of American teenage girls disagree with their parents about sex. 192

24% of Americans think only women should be nurses. 244

24% of Americans think of God as a cross between a mother figure and a father figure. 116

25%

25% of Americans think the sun is a planet. 254

25% of Americans consider themselves very religious. 252

25% of Americans think their presence at a sporting event will influence its outcome. 117

25% of American adults bowl. *112*

25% of American adults never exercise at all. 267

25% of American mothers gain at least 36 pounds during pregnancy. 178

25% of American large-size women have trouble finding bras of suitable size and style. 124

25% of Americans never think about women's rights. 119

25% of American men strongly support the women's movement. 223

25% of American banana-eaters eat less than ⅖ of a banana at each sitting. 288

25% of American AIDS victims were intravenous drug users. 206

25% of Americans aged 18 to 25 have used cocaine. 206

25% of American arsonists are under 15 years of age. 101

25% of Americans aged 8 to 17 think that when both mothers and fathers work outside of the home, it has a good effect on children 12 and under. 246

25% of American households are touched by crime each year. 210

25% of American television news anchors don't care very much about watching television. 126

25% of Americans have hardly any confidence in the press. 151

25% of Americans think poor people live well on welfare. 171

25% of Americans think Social Security should provide by itself a retirement income sufficient for a comfortable standard of living. 201

25% of Americans think the current rate of growth of science and technology in America is too fast. 245

25% of American commercial airline accidents are caused by weather. 217

25% of Americans could be killed within 30 days by a large Soviet nuclear attack if urban populations were evacuated from risk areas. 233

25% of American wives would object to their daughter's having premarital intercourse. 115

25% of American teenage girls think war is inevitable. 202

26%

26% of American women aged 19 to 30 have gone on binges of eating large quantities of high-calorie food in a short period of time. 111

26% of American teenage girls who have asked a boy out let him pay for the date. 192

26% of American women enjoy sex more than money. 117

26% of American husbands would agree to pay their wives a weekly salary. 193

26% of American murder victims are female. 210

26% of American families are headed by a single parent. 117

26% of American pregnancies end in abortion. 102

26% of Americans aged 8 to 17 have four living grandparents. 246

26% of Americans think the American steel industry has declined because of highly paid union workers. 201

26% of American wastepaper is recovered and reused. 112

26% of American pharmaceutical drugs treat the central nervous system. 190

26% of American teenage girls have normal skin. 159

26% of American females aged 15 to 21 who own a car have a boyfriend who does the maintenance or repairs. 181

26% of Americans think most poor people are lazy. 171

26% of Americans think housework is risky. 113

26% of Americans are injured each year. 112

26% of American women are afraid that AIDS can be caught by casual contact, such as working or attending school with an infected person. 229

26% of American wives never masturbate. 115

26% of American fourth-graders have tried alcohol. 220

26% of Americans would be unwilling to increase their taxes for day-care programs. 212

26% of Americans think Wall Street insider trading is simply people making money because they know more than other people (and should not be illegal). 235

26% of American men think the old ways are still the best ways. 223

26% of Americans think God can be thought of as both a friend and a king. 116

26% of Americans often eat apples. 287

26% of Americans who are admitted to a hospital for psychiatric reasons are committed. 255

27%

27% of American teenage girls bought at least ten pairs of shoes and boots in the last year. 179

27% of American teenage girls intend to purchase more shoes next year than they did this year. 179

27% of American teenage girls disagree with their parents about clothing. 192

27% of American 17-year-old Hispanics do not know Hitler was the leader of Germany during World War II. 207

27% of American men aged 18 to 44 cannot identify any situation that would lead them to enlist and fight for their country. 222

27% of American abortions are performed on women under 20 years of age. 112

27% of Americans think that if abortions were made illegal the moral tone of America would improve. 201

27% of American high school seniors have shoplifted in the last year. 210

27% of American women would respect a man less if he became a househusband. 193

27% of American husbands never throw so much as a dirty sock into the washer. 197

27% of American teenage girls use bubble bath. 169

27% of American women think they would do better than average in a fistfight. 117

27% of Americans have been affected, or know someone personally close to them who has been affected, by floods. 231

27% of Americans aged 8 to 17 think their parents place too little emphasis on cultural activities, such as going to museums and classical music events. 246

27% of American households burn wood. 136

27% of American women of child-bearing age use the pill for contraception. 229

27% of Americans think divorce should be easier to obtain. 119

28%

28% of American babies are born, in their parents' estimation, at the wrong time. 112

28% of Americans who die in nursing homes lived there less than a month. 133

28% of American medical degrees are conferred on women. 112

28% of Americans aged 50 to 64 think children should be sure their elderly parents have adequate income. 201

28% of American liberals have gone skinny-dipping. 117

28% of American lawyers think social hosts should bear legal liability for accidents caused by drunken guests. 141

28% of American inmates of state prisons live in housing units with less than 40 square feet. 210

28% of Americans are not served by sewer systems. 112

28% of American men consider themselves handsome. 117

28% of Americans boat. 112

28% of American high school seniors have cut school in the last four weeks. 271

28% of Americans think honest people are honest because they're afraid of being caught in a dishonest act. 114

28% of Americans are Catholic. 112

28% of Americans think that their job is very exciting. 128

28% of Americans would love to try parachuting out of an airplane. 128

28% of Americans have taken prescription medicine in the last 24 hours. 153

28% of Americans think the benefits to society of technological and scientific innovation in the next 20 years will not outweigh the risks. 245

28% of Americans think their own basic understanding of science and technology is poor. 245

29%

29% of Americans would not take a test that indicated whether they were likely to develop a fatal disease later in life. 245

29% of Americans think that a doctor who advertises is in effect saying that he isn't very successful. 131

29% of American 3-year-olds are enrolled in school. 112

29% of American single women have not become more cautious about sex because of fear of AIDS. 229

29% of American casino game winnings are made at the craps tables. 205

29% of American brides are first married at age 25 or older. 200

29% of American teenage girls have had sexual intercourse. 192

29% of Americans disapprove of the government's providing birth control services for teenagers. 212

29% of American teenage girls do not plan to work after having children. 192

29% of Americans want their boss's job. 117

29% of Americans think women should take care of running their home and leave running the country to men. 119

29% of Americans think the government should reduce the difference in income between people with high and low incomes. 119

29% of Americans think communism is a bad form of government, but no worse than others. 150

29% of American deportable aliens who are located have been previously expelled from America. 112

29% of Americans think the SDI, or "Star Wars" missile defense system, will be harmful to national security. 240

29% of Americans have had visions. 269

29% of American teenage boys worry about losing their hair. 117

29% of Americans have been moved to tears by a greeting card. 117

29% of America is forest land. 112

29% of Americans feel magazines that show nudity should be totally banned. 110

30%

30% of American 17-year-olds think the Spanish Armada was destroyed in the Spanish-American War. 207

30% of Americans think there should be more Hispanics in the army. 119

30% of American women aged 19 to 39 believe their life would be better if they were thinner. 111

30% of American teenage girls intend to live with a man before marriage. 192

30% of American women who are murdered are done in by husbands or boyfriends. 101

30% of American women think being a wife is the best thing about being a woman. 249

30% of American murderers convicted in US District Court are not imprisoned. 112

30% of Americans think the IRS should not go after people who get paid in cash and do not report it as income. 244

30% of Americans think publishing pamphlets to protest against the government should not be allowed. 119

30% of Americans who buy a new American car buy one with power seats. 256

30% of Americans sometimes or never avoid driving after drinking. 231

30% of American assault victims took no self-protective actions. 194

30% of American teeth in 17-year-olds are decayed, filled, or missing. 163

30% of American households have central air conditioning. 136

30% of American teenage girls feel homosexuality is an acceptable alternative life-style. 192

30% of Americans have visited Yellowstone National Park. 117

30% of Americans smoke cigarettes. 102

30% of Americans aged 18 to 44 say they were opposed to the political agitators of the 1960s and early 1970s. 222

30% of Americans think a Vietnamese boat refugee who was persecuted at home for associating with American policy should not be admitted to America. 121

30% of Americans, if they had the ability, would love to try singing a solo on the stage at the Grand Ole Opry. 128

30% of Americans like musical spirituals. 236

30% of American men think everything is changing too fast today. 223

30% of Americans, even if there was no direct risk to humans, would disapprove of genetic manipulation to make larger game fish. 245

31%

31% of Americans think it best for the future of America if we stay out of world affairs. 119

31% of Americans who travel overseas travel alone. 213

31% of American physicians do not think the high quality of health care in the United States justifies its high cost. 131

31% of American physicians think not-for-profit hospitals provide better quality care than for-profit hospitals. 131

31% of American companies have a member of an ethnic minority on their board of directors. 215

31% of American blacks live below the poverty line. 112

31% of American teenage girls have a regular allowance. 248

31% of American fifth-graders have tried wine coolers. 220

31% of American women cannot imagine a situation in which they would approve of a policeman striking a man. 210

31% of Americans aged 8 to 17 have no brothers. 246

31% of Americans arrested for prostitution and commercialized vice are male. 210

31% of American women think the man should pay for every date. 193

31% of American women aged 15 to 44 had sexual intercourse for the first time the month of their marriage. 112

31% of Americans think organizing protest marches and demonstrations against the government should not be allowed. *119*

31% of Americans think the reading of the Lord's Prayer or Bible verses should be required in public schools. 119

31% of Americans think that, generally speaking, government is the answer. 150

31% of Americans do not think it is an honor to serve in government. 252

31% of Americans do not really believe in getting as much fun out of life as possible. 252

32%

32% of American 17-year-olds do not know what the Declaration of Independence was for. 207

32% of American arguments between parents are over disciplining children. 107

32% of Americans think the use of genetically engineered organisms in the environment will likely change rainfall patterns. 245

32% of American women would like to alter their bust. 116

32% of Americans are very likely to become organ donors. 117

32% of Americans bicycle. 112

32% of Americans oppose the 55-mile-per-hour speed limit. 210

32% of America is owned by the Federal Government. 112

32% of American whites think that if an equally qualified white and black are competing for a job, the black is more likely to be hired. 281

32% of Americans think that, of the last ten presidents, Kennedy could be trusted most in a crisis. 237

32% of American lawyers have advertised their services at some point. 138

32% of American entertainment celebrities say they read their reviews but don't take critics seriously. 130

32% of Americans find shopping an unpleasant experience. *252*

32% of American rabbis believe that secular humanism has a good impact on the country. 266

32% of American high school seniors do not think servicemen should obey orders without question. 271

32% of Americans like to take chances. 252

33%

33% of Americans think watching TV is the best way to spend an evening. 110

33% of Americans with children in the home do not hope the children have a life-style much like their own. 283

33% of Americans think convicted heroin dealers should get the death penalty. 210

33% of American rape victims used or tried physical force against their attacker. 194.

33% of Americans think women in the armed forces should be used in hand-to-hand combat. 119

33% of Americans have a great deal of confidence in the military. 114

33% of Americans think everyone should be given an income large enough to provide a decent life for his family, no matter his work. 119

33% of American women are concerned about wrinkles. 116

33% of American youth do not think cigarette smoking poses a great health risk. 102

33% of Americans have tried marijuana at least once in their life. 251

33% of Americans have stayed up past midnight in the last 24 hours. 153

33% of Americans think that the leaders of the environmental movement are unreasonable in their criticism and demands. 245

33% of Americans think robots and automation will worsen the quality of life for people like themselves. 245

33% of Americans would have little or no interest in being transported 100 years into the future. 128

33% of Americans have never had a *déjà vu*. 119

33% of American women are not very much concerned with fashion. 125

33% of American men spend more than 45 minutes each day on their looks. 223

34%

34% of American high school seniors often feel lonely. 153

34% of American adults fish. 112

34% of American teenage girls own ice skates. 204

34% of American women would like to change their legs. 116

34% of American men aged 17 to 21 are a friend of their partner when they first have intercourse. 277

34% of American brides are first married under the age of 21. 200

34% of American gentiles wouldn't want their children marrying Jews. 152

34% of Americans aged 8 to 17 say their home life would be better if their family had more money. 246

34% of Americans do not go out to dinner in an average week. 252

34% of American households have microwave ovens. 112

34% of American car thefts occur in parking lots. 210

34% of Americans held up by an unarmed robber are injured. 194

34% of American lawyers think social hosts have an obligation to prevent their guests from getting drunk. 141

34% of Americans have gone to the movies in the last month. 111

34% of Americans who do not always wear seatbelts do not because in the event of an accident they want to be able to get out of the car quickly. 231

34% of Americans on Death Row have no prior felony convictions. 210

34% of American teenage girls use a hair coloring. 162

34% of American counterfeiters are female. 101

35%

35% of American chefs and restaurant owners are overweight. 127

35% of Americans go out for dinner once in an average week. 252

35% of Americans who eat candy are likely to give candy as a Christmas gift. 191

35% of American women would like to lose at least 25 pounds. 116

35% of American endangered species are birds. 112

35% of American college men say they might commit a rape if there was no chance of getting caught. 117

35% of Americans aged 8 to 17 have no sisters. 246

35% of American single parents have no problem spending enough time with their children. 212

35% of Americans have been affected, or know someone personally close to them who has been affected, by exposure to toxic chemicals. 231

35% of American men who work part-time are heavy drinkers. 250

35% of Americans abstain from the use of alcohol. 102

35% of married Americans would not like to learn to play a musical instrument. 195.

35% of Americans generally find advertising enjoyable. 261

35% of Americans who gamble on a regular basis think gambling is very risky. 231

35% of American teenagers who attend evangelical churches have sexual intercourse before the age of 17. 198

35% of Americans have been punched or beaten. 119

36%

36% of American adults have 21 or more decayed, filled, or missing teeth. 163

36% of American men would like to change their teeth. 116

36% of American men would like to change their hair. 116

36% of American teenage girls worry about losing their hair. 117

36% of American women executives say that wearing perfume helps a woman's career. 117

36% of American women think power and influence are of no importance in fulfilling their personal goals. 229

36% of Americans are involved in a charity or social service activity. 110

36% of American households have a VCR. 112

36% of American inmates who die in jail die of natural causes. 210

36% of Americans on Death Row have been there for over four years. 112

36% of American teenage girls favor the death penalty. 202

36% of Americans who have used alcohol say they have had a problem with it in the past. 103

36% of Americans strongly believe people should be allowed to take whatever risks they want as long as they don't endanger or bother others. 231

36% of American supermarket shoppers buy items from the salad bar. 116

36% of Americans generally conform to custom and avoid the unconventional. 252

36% of Americans think that the contribution that a major company makes to the economy as a whole is more important than the stake of the stockholders. 230

36% of Americans who earn the minimum wage or less are 19 years old or younger. 186

36% of American women corporate officers associate boats with success. 149

36% of American embezzlers are female. 101

37%

37% of Americans who believe in life after death think it will be filled with intense action. 119

37% of American wives always play an active part in sex. 115

37% of American women say their biggest sports thrill would be to get the winning hit in the World Series. 117

37% of American women would like to change their teeth. 116

37% of American working women wear a larger size top than pants. 123

37% of American women prefer to adopt a fashion after it has won some acceptance. 125

37% of American divorced and widowed men like getting advice from women on their grooming. 223

37% of Americans think a person advocating government ownership of big industries should not be allowed to teach in a university. 119

37% of Americans think the government should control prices. 119

37% of Americans think a man from England who wants to start a new life for himself here should not be admitted to America. 121

37% of Americans think premarital sex is always or almost always wrong. 114

37% of Americans aged 12 and above have used an illicit drug. 206

37% of Americans think beer brewed in Germany is of lower quality than beer brewed in America. 252

37% of American households have vegetable gardens. 112

37% of Americans favor removing from the public library books opposing churches and religion. 119

37% of American garbage is paper and paperboard. 112

37% of Americans who would refuse to buy stock on an insider tip would because it's wrong to do it. 234

37% of Americans who would refuse to buy stock on an insider tip would because the tip might not be any good. 234

38%

38% of American entertainment celebrities think their public image does not correspond with what they are like privately. 130

38% of American entertainment celebrities think their public image corresponds with what they are like privately. 130

38% of American teenage girls feel homosexuality is an illness, but not a sin. 192

38% of Americans die of heart disease. 112

38% of Americans think doctors act as if they're better than other people. 131

38% of American households have dishwashers. 112

38% of American women corporate officers rate themselves as accomplished chefs. 149

38% of Americans have skipped breakfast in the last 24 hours. 153

38% of American wives who have never had an extramarital experience have had a strong desire to do so. 115

38% of American women would like to improve their buttocks. 116

38% of Americans think only men should be airline pilots. 244

38% of American commercial airline accidents are caused by pilot error. 217

38% of American women would be afraid to leave their child at a day-care center. 229

38% of Americans dislike rock music. 236

38% of Americans think the Bible is the actual word of God and is to be taken literally, word for word. 119

38% of American teenage girls learned about menstruation from a book or booklet. 161

39%

39% of American teenage girls argue with their parents about boyfriends. 192

39% of American murders occur after arguments. 112

39% of American households own a dog. 154

39% of American babies are first-born. 112

39% of American lawyers feel AIDS victims can lawfully be denied access to public schools. 144

39% of Americans say they are in excellent health. 134

39% of Americans often drink tea. 287

39% of American shoppers frequently make an unplanned impulse-purchase at the grocery store. 247

39% of Americans often eat ice cream. 287

39% of American teenage girls think an unhappily married couple should get divorced even if they have children. 202

39% of Americans are afraid to walk alone at night in areas within a mile of their homes. 151

39% of Americans never go to the movies. 117

39% of Americans think the government should spend less on culture and the arts. 119

39% of Americans think people with high incomes should pay the same percentage of their earnings in taxes as those who earn low incomes. 119

39% of American corporate executives think the business community is doing a fair or poor job at providing equal pay for equal work. 259

39% of American jail inmates are unconvicted. 112

39% of American wives never discuss their intimate sexual feelings and desires with anyone. 115

39% of American fifth-graders say they are in love. *117*

39% of Americans who live alone are aged 65 and older. 112

39% of Americans do not think that an honest person is necessarily a good person. 252

40%

40% of Americans think comparable worth is a better way to determine how much a job pays than is supply and demand. 264

40% of American high school seniors think that if things are just left to God they will turn out for the best. 271

40% of American wives 40 years old and older have had an extramarital affair. 115

40% of Americans first learned about sex from friends. 116

40% of American wives often perform fellatio on their husbands. 115

40% of American fifth-graders have felt peer pressure to try wine coolers. 220

40% of Americans have had a pizza delivered in the last three months. 117

40% of Americans do not think a college education is important to succeed in the business world. 252

40% of American high school students identify Israel as an Arab nation. 117

40% of Americans have attended a church or synagogue in the last week. 110

40% of Americans think some numbers are especially lucky for some people. 270

40% of Americans think homosexuals should not be hired into the armed forces. 152

40% of Americans think that, generally speaking, government is the problem. 150

40% of Americans say they are honest in what they say and do some of the time. 252

40% of Americans who oppose the death penalty for convicted murders do so because they think it is wrong to take a life. 210

40% of Americans, when they have leisure time, do not really like to take it easy. 252

40% of American male prison inmates were unemployed when they entered prison. 194

40% of Americans, if they had the ability, would like to try arguing a case before the Supreme Court. 128

41%

41% of American white TV evangelical followers think TV evangelical preachers do more harm than good. 242

41% of American teenage girls own a television set. 204

41% of American adults are missing seven or more teeth. 163

41% of Americans have cereal for breakfast. 120

41% of American women do not own a skirt. 125

41% of Americans feel it is important that they are well dressed at all times. 252

41% of American women think the father should have the right to veto an abortion. 193

41% of Americans think only men should be police officers. 244

41% of American working mothers with young children leave them with family during the day. 193

41% of Americans believe a person who claims blacks are genetically inferior should be allowed to teach in a university. 119

41% of Americans do not think schools are giving children an interest in learning. 212

41% of Americans aged 8 to 17 would grade most of their teachers an "A." 246

41% of Americans do not think most people can be trusted. 119

41% of American women 65 years old and older live alone. 112

41% of American prisoners live in single-occupancy units. 194

41% of Americans on Death Row were never married. 112

41% of Americans have felt as though they were really in touch with someone who had died. 119

41% of Americans think business as a whole is making too much profit. 258

41% of Americans think rocket launchings and other space activities have caused changes in our weather. 270

42%

42% of Americans have not been to the dentist in the last year. 134

42% of American women do not own a girdle. 125

42% of American teenage girls think movies have gone too far in showing nudity. 202

42% of American workers say their boss has a big or outrageous ego. 232

42% of American women think there will be a black president by the year 2000. 229

42% of Americans on Death Row are black. 112

42% of American murder victims are black. 210

42% of American accidents occur at home. 134

42% of American motor vehicle deaths are alcohol-related. 206

42% of American adults watch the late news on TV. 112

42% of Americans cannot name a country near the Pacific Ocean. 117

42% of American households have indoor houseplants. 112

42% of Americans haven't decided if they support or oppose nuclear power plants. 113

42% of Americans think a child should be physically punished if he is deliberately destructive. 106

42% of Americans think homosexuals should not be allowed to teach in a university. 119

42% of Americans think that if the military draft were reinstated, married people should be exempted. 119

42% of Americans think the churches are doing a fair or poor job in meeting their responsibilities to children. 212

43%

43% of American girls aged 15 to 19 who have never married have had sexual intercourse. 112

43% of American women aged 21 to 35 think the women's movement led to a weakening of traditional moral values. 122

43% of American women do not think women should call men for a date. 193

43% of American lawyers have done 25 or fewer hours of pro bono work in the last year. 145

43% of American physicians think there are too many physicians in their community. 131

43% of American robbers do not use weapons. 101

43% of Americans think nuclear power will worsen the quality of life for people like themselves. 245

43% of Americans think it is likely that some UFOs are really space vehicles from other civilizations. 270

43% of Americans think that the government must see to it that everyone has a job and that prices are stable, even if it means restricting the rights of businessmen. 119

43% of Americans think the government should limit the profits companies make. 263

43% of American 17-year-old girls do not know Watergate occurred after 1950. 207

43% of Americans think a person has a right to commit suicide if he has an incurable disease. 119

43% of American male shoppers go to the supermarket three or more times a week. 257

43% of Americans watch daytime TV almost every day. 252

43% of Americans think they exercise enough. 275

43% of Americans who have no religion feel close to God most of the time. 164

43% of Americans do not feel that a person who is religious is also more likely to be an honest person. 252

44%

44% of American women think they would have gone further in the world if they were men. 193

44% of American teenage girls use shaving cream or lotion. 161

44% of American mothers say they are more in love with their partner since becoming a parent. 276

44% of Americans are not really happier than they were five years ago. 252

44% of American adults go to their parents for advice on important personal decisions. 104

44% of American adults participate in flower gardening. 112

44% of American households have a gun. 116

44% of American teenage girls have asked a boy for a date. 192

44% of American teenage girls think teenage values on sexual freedom today are too liberal. 202

44% of American women think the AIDS crisis encourages men and women to marry. 229

44% of Americans like rock music. 236

44% of Americans cannot name a significant contribution made to America by immigrants. 116

44% of American patents are issued to residents of other countries. 112

44% of Americans live in states with populations of over 10 million. 112

44% of Americans think people who sue physicians for malpractice are usually just looking for an easy way to make some money. 131

44% of American independent pet stores sell reptiles and amphibians. 156

44% of Americans would not like members of religious sects or cults as neighbors. 152

44% of Americans believe that God created man pretty much in his present form at one time within the past 10,000 years. 183

45%

45% of American robbery victims take no self-protective actions. 194

45% of Americans who own stock have a portfolio worth under $5000. 225

45% of American teenage girls play backgammon. 177

45% of American grocery stores use scanning checkouts. 247

45% of American women abstain from the use of alcohol. 102

45% of Americans think that abortion should be permitted during the first three months of pregnancy. 110

45% of Americans think that abortion should be illegal. 110

45% of American women corporate officers do not feel they have had to give something up to be successful. 149

45% of Americans think it's a bad idea for older people to share a home with their grown children. 119

45% of American women have very little or no confidence in politicians. 229

45% of Americans expect America to fight in another world war within the next 10 years. 119

45% of Americans have been affected, or know someone personally close to them who has been affected, by tornadoes or hurricanes. 231

45% of Americans live within 15 minutes of their best friend. 119

45% of Americans who have been divorced think their ex-spouse is happier now than before the divorce. 109

45% of American women weigh 140 pounds or more. 279

45% of American women wear uncomfortable shoes because they look good. 117

45% of American men consider shopping an unpleasant experience. 252

45% of Americans committed to psychiatric institutions are schizophrenics. 255

45% of Americans who buy a new American car buy one with power windows. 256

45% of American owners of small businesses are children of owners of small businesses. 265

45% of American men are strongly satisfied with how they look in the nude. 223

45% of American divorced and widowed men think people are losing touch with each other. 223

46%

46% of Americans think we have no business meddling with nature. 245

46% of American women would like to change their thighs. 116

46% of American men think the armed forces are unfair to women. 193

46% of Americans think judges should use probation for women offenders as an alternative to prison. 210

46% of Americans say they don't know how they'd get along without Scotch tape. 117

46% of Americans think that when the SDI, or "Star Wars" missile defense system, is fully developed, it will not work. 240

46% of Americans believe in life on other planets. 269

46% of Americans say they suffer great stress at least once a week. 267

46% of Americans think the country is spending too much money on welfare. 150

46% of Americans think people who have lived in America illegally for several years should be deported. 210

46% of Americans think cars assembled in Japan are of lower quality than cars assembled in America. 252

46% of Americans think the use of genetically engineered organisms in the environment will likely mutate into a deadly disease. 245

46% of Americans who report to a supervisor at work would be uncomfortable discussing having hemorrhoids with him. 253

46% of Americans think homosexuals should not be hired as doctors. 152

46% of American leading medical experts think a vaccine for AIDS will be available before the turn of the century. 218

46% of Americans, even if they had the ability, would have little or no interest in writing a novel. 128

46% of American women think the private lives of political figures should be of concern to voters. 229

46% of Americans say television news portrays politicians too favorably. 117

46% of Americans sight-see. 112

46% of Americans who are regular smokers have not quit because they've tried to quit but can't do it right now. 231

46% of Americans have never smoked. 112

46% of Americans feel the single greatest happiness is good health. 252

47%

47% of Americans generally find advertising annoying. 261

47% of Americans find TV advertising the most annoying advertising. 261

47% of Americans have felt as though they were very close to a powerful spiritual force that seemed to lift them out of themselves. 119

47% of Americans believe sexually explicit books, magazines, and movies can help improve the sex lives of some couples. 116

47% of American women do not think sex before marriage is acceptable. 229

47% of American parents say they are less strict than their own parents were. 106

47% of American men enjoy sex more than money. 117

47% of American women aged 21 to 35 think that the opportunity to achieve a fulfilling life is more available to men than women. 122

47% of American women aged 21 to 35 think the women's movement made many women go out and get a job when they would probably be happier at home. 122

47% of American women think a man reaches his prime during his thirties. 193

47% of Americans think their weight is just right. 275

47% of Americans 65 years old or older have arthritis. 112

47% of Americans wear eyeglasses. 112

47% of Americans favor local laws banning the sale and possession of handguns. 110

47% of Americans oppose local laws banning the sale and possession of handguns. 110

47% of American women frequently look for brand or designer names when shopping for clothes. 125

47% of American men like getting all dressed up for dates or special occasions. 223

47% of Americans do not think that homosexual relations between consenting adults should be legal. 111

48%

48% of American teenage girls would consider marrying a man of a different race if they loved him. 202

48% of American blacks think life is worse now than it was when they were growing up. 212

48% of Americans with children in the home think a home without children can be as fulfilling as one with them. 283

48% of American astronauts have experienced motion sickness in space. 117

48% of Americans drive for pleasure. 112

48% of Americans sometimes or never drive at or below the speed limit. 231

48% of American females often feel guilty after eating candy. 191

48% of American teenage girls have had blackheads in the last month. 159

48% of Americans prefer not to work around people who smoke cigarettes. 152

48% of American smokers favor a ban on tobacco advertising. 175

48% of American teenage girls own a class ring. 176

48% of Americans often sing, hum, or whistle. 117

48% of Americans picnic. 112

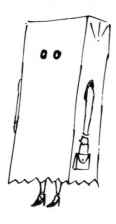

48% of American women would like to cover the signs of aging. 116

48% of Americans often eat tomatoes. 287

48% of American farmers have lived on their farms for at least ten years. 112

48% of Americans think the bad effects of credit cards outweigh the good. 113

48% of directors of large American corporations think corporate merger and acquisition activity has hurt the American economy. 132

48% of American income tax returns are filed jointly. 112

48% of American leading medical implant scientists think artificial breasts will be more widely used in the year 2000 than they are now. 218

48% of American men believe looks, not brains, are what women judge them by. 223

49%

49% of Americans think of God as a redeemer. 116

49% of American teenage girls send Easter cards. 167

49% of American casino game winnings are made at the blackjack tables. 205

49% of American chefs and restaurant owners think the most outstanding examples of American food are steak or hamburger. 127

49% of American men would like to trim their waistlines. 116

49% of American women think it is acceptable for a single woman to have and raise children. 193

49% of American 4-year-olds are enrolled in school. 112

49% of American women aged 15 to 44 who are divorced or widowed remarry within five years. 112

49% of Americans think companies should be allowed to make all the profits they can. 263

49% of Americans think unions increase the chance that companies will go out of business. 116

49% of American blacks think that most blacks work harder than most whites. 281

49% of Americans think doctors don't care about people as much as they used to. 175

49% of American high school seniors think cocaine is easy to come by. 210

49% of American women have bought a floral arrangement for a funeral in the last year. 203

49% of Americans want to live to 100. 117

49% of American raw-onion eaters eat no more than one slice at a sitting. 288

49% of American teenage girls use liquid mouthwash. 161

50%

50% of American households do not purchase ice cream. 284

50% of American marriages do not last seven years. 112

50% of American men think the father should have the right to veto an abortion. 193

50% of American murders are committed with a handgun. 194

50% of Americans who murder law enforcement officers are black. 210

50% of Americans believe the accused are guilty until proven innocent. 117

50% of Americans think quotas to increase the number of minority students in colleges should be illegal. 153

50% of American residents who are foreign-born are not citizens. 112

50% of American men are less than 5'9" tall. 280

50% of Americans think jogging is risky. 113

50% of Americans eat three meals a day. 274

50% of American wives who have had extramarital sex have had only one lover. 115

50% of American fruit-pie eaters eat less than one entire slice per sitting. 288

50% of American teenage girls get money from their parents when they need it. 248

50% of American women think carrying a handgun for self-defense is justified. 229

50% of American women aged 65 or older are widows. 196

50% of Americans do not feel the way a person dresses is an indication of his success. 252

50% of Americans do not read books. 112

50% of Americans read books. 112

51%

51% of the American fish catch is made within three miles of shore. 112

51% of Americans feel our form of government is admired by people throughout the world. 252

51% of American dollars that are gambled are played at casino tables. 205

51% of Americans strongly believe avoiding risk is mainly the responsiblity of the individual. 231

51% of Americans feel they have little control over the risks faced in daily living. 113

51% of Americans aged 13 to 17 think schools should have the right to search students' lockers, belongings, or cars for drugs or liquor. 246

51% of American high school seniors have used marijuana. 206

51% of Americans aged 18 to 25 think most young people today don't have enough discipline. 252

51% of Americans never go to a bar or tavern. 119

51% of Americans often drink coffee. 287

51% of Americans have sought a second opinion from another doctor. 227

51% of Americans are more worried by someone who might be too eager for an arms control agreement than by someone who might not be working hard enough for one. 150

51% of American high school seniors go out with a date at least once a week. 153

51% of American adults watch the early news on TV. 112

51% of Americans buy generic products. 116

51% of American women think surrogate motherhood should be prohibited. 229

52%

52% of Americans think the use of genetically engineered organisms in the environment will likely endanger the food supply. 245

52% of American Girl Scouts are Brownies. 112

52% of American men feel people are so caught up in making a living that they lose track of what is important in life. 223

52% of Americans daydream about being rich. 117

52% of American men think a divorced woman should pay alimony to her former husband in some situations. 193

52% of American shoppers think it is extremely important that a grocery store offer double-value coupons. 247

52% of American men are willing to pay top dollar to get high quality. 223

52% of American men think a woman reaches her prime during her thirties. 193

52% of American fruit and vegetable imports come from Latin America. 208

52% of Americans live within 50 miles of the coastal shorelines. 112

52% of American workers live within 20 minutes of work. 118

52% of Americans killed in railroad accidents were on a road crossing the tracks. 112

52% of Americans used a seatbelt last time they got into a car. 110

52% of American households have two or more motor vehicles. 112

52% of Americans would have little or no interest in parachuting out of an airplane. 128

52% of Americans feel society should restrict certain hazardous activities and products, even if the restrictions limit individual freedoms. 113

52% of Americans think everyone should have a blood test for AIDS. 285

52% of Americans think people generally depend on them for ideas and opinions. 252

52% of Americans aged 13 to 17 believe in astrology. 268

53%

53% of Americans think blacks shouldn't push themselves where they're not wanted. 119

53% of American black children live with one parent. 185

53% of American blacks think blacks are paid less than whites for doing the same job. 281

53% of Americans want the Federal Government to have less influence on the educational program of local schools. 110

53% of Americans have had, or know someone personally close to them who has had, a serious automobile accident. 231

53% of Americans walk for pleasure. 112

53% of Americans of voting age voted in the presidential election of 1984. 112

53% of Americans held up by a robber armed with a stick or bottle are injured. 194

53% of Americans have had joint pain in the last year. 267

53% of Americans who are issued passports are female. 213

53% of American babies are breast-fed. 112

53% of American companies have a woman on their board of directors. 215

53% of Americans would disapprove of scientists changing the makeup of human cells to improve the intelligence level that children would inherit. 245

53% of American high school seniors agree with their parents about things it's OK to do when they're on a date. 153

53% of Americans think the Soviet Union is an evil empire that threatens our moral and religious values. 165

54%

54% of American white TV evangelical followers think TV evangelical preachers are in it mainly for the money they raise from their followers. 242

54% of Americans think a person who speaks against churches and religion should not be allowed to teach in a university. 119

54% of Americans think there is much goodness in the world which hints at God's goodness. 164

54% of American men say the most satisfying accomplishment for a man is to be a father. 223

54% of American women aged 21 to 35 think the women's movement made it harder to hold marriages together. 122

54% of Americans think pornography leads people to commit rape. 119

54% of American robberies are committed at night. 210

54% of American women think that whoever asks for a date should pay for it. 193

54% of American women think that a divorced woman with an adequate salary should not receive alimony. 193

54% of American children in female-headed households live in poverty. 150

54% of Americans feel the family is disappearing from American life. 252

54% of American convicted murderers use alcohol just before committing the crime. 250

54% of Americans do not often do things on the spur of the moment. 252

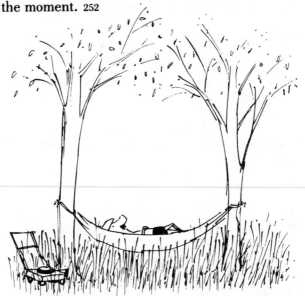

54% of Americans think mowing the lawn is risky. *113*

54% of American migrant farmworkers travel 500 miles or more to reach their jobs. 278

54% of American women think America should not intervene either militarily or economically in the affairs of other countries. 229

54% of Americans think that as a result of federal deregulation, job safety, environmental quality, and product safety have all declined. 241

54% of Americans think the Federal Government has too much power. 119

55%

55% of Americans would have little or no interest in hosting the Johnny Carson show. 128

55% of American playground injuries occur on the monkey bars. 117

55% of American fathers say they are more in love with their partner since becoming a parent. 276

55% of American women corporate officers feel they have had to give something up to be successful. 149

55% of Americans think a preschool child is likely to suffer if his mother works. 119

55% of Americans prefer American food when they eat out. 116

55% of Americans say they would not accept a job if a lie detector test were required. 117

55% of Americans say they are honest in what they say and do all of the time. 252

55% of Americans think that nearly everyone who has a chance cheats somewhat on income tax. 114

55% of Americans say they would take an illegal insider tip and buy stock to make money. 235

55% of Americans think most people become millionaires because of the family they are born into and the people they know. 153

55% of Americans say religion is very important in their lives. 110

55% of Americans often eat eggs. 287

55% of Americans, even if they had the ability, would have little or no interest in racing a car at the Indy 500. 128

55% of Americans, if given the chance, would not travel to outer space. 113

55% of Americans think the increase in nonpublic schools is a good thing for the nation. 165

55% of Americans think that the people running the country don't really care what happens to them. 116

55% of Americans think the Soviet Union is becoming a more trustworthy nation. 240

55% of Americans think laws should be changed to make immigration more difficult. 210

55% of Americans who move relocate in the same county. 112

55% of Americans who would be troubled if the universe were expanding feel that way because God's creation would be coming undone. 254

56%

56% of American lawyers feel they don't make enough money. 143

56% of American murder victims are white. 210

56% of American trials in US District Court have no juries. 112

56% of Americans favor a complete ban on smoking in public places. 152

56% of American physicians favor a ban on the advertising of all alcoholic beverages. 175

56% of Americans are not skeptical about most claims in advertising. 252

56% of Americans are at their best in the morning. 117

56% of Americans approve of surrogate motherhood if the child is raised by a married woman who is infertile. 105

56% of Americans have had a backache in the last year. 267

56% of American women corporate officers think being a woman has made success harder to attain. 149

56% of American women do not think there will be a woman president by the year 2000. 229

56% of American teenage girls are concerned about being alone. 192

56% of American high school seniors first used alcohol before the tenth grade. 250

56% of Americans think the educational standards in schools are poor. 150

56% of American lawyers oppose a balanced budget amendment to the Constitution. 139

56% of Americans think it is the responsibility of government to meet everyone's needs, even in case of sickness, poverty, unemployment, and old age. 119

57%

57% of Americans think pornography breaks down morals. 119

57% of Americans are not comfortable unless their home is neat and clean. 252

57% of American white TV evangelical followers do not think white TV evangelical preachers are real moral forces, the kind of religious leaders the country needs. 242

57% of Americans think the justice system favors the rich. 210

57% of American women believe in love at first sight. 117

57% of Americans pray at least once a day. 119

57% of Americans are Protestant. 112

57% of American coal comes from surface mines. 112

57% of Americans think that since they were children physical abuse of children by parents has increased. 212

57% of Americans think the use of genetically engineered organisms in the environment will likely produce birth defects in humans. 245

57% of Americans favor urine tests for students. 103

57% of American women think men can have a happy and complete life without getting married. 193

57% of American women think that when they marry they give up more freedom than men do. 193

57% of American households have a pet. 116

57% of Americans have seen someone buy something he should not have with food stamps. 171

57% of American motorcyclists who die in accidents are intoxicated. 250

57% of Americans think they look younger than they are. 117

57% of American cheese is American cheese. 112

58%

58% of American college graduates eat candy at least once a week. 191

58% of American high school seniors have used illicit drugs. 206

58% of American high school seniors rate themselves as above average in intelligence. 271

58% of American high school seniors would like to stay in the same job for most of their adult life. 153

58% of Americans think hostile takeovers of companies have done more harm than good to the American economy. 230

58% of Americans are not concerned about getting AIDS. 286

58% of Americans believe religion can answer all or most of today's problems. 110

58% of Americans think that if the military draft were reinstated, conscientious objectors should not be exempted. 119

58% of Americans see God as a judge. 116

58% of American men think self-sufficient women are more appealing. 193

58% of American runaways are female. 101

58% of Americans think blacks have worse jobs, income, and housing than whites because they just don't have the motivation or will power to pull themselves up out of poverty. 119

58% of Americans who regularly smoke in bed think it is very risky. 231

58% of Americans like stuffed peppers. 116

58% of Americans who report to a supervisor at work would be uncomfortable discussing having constipation with him. 253

58% of Americans who contract gonorrhea are male. 219

58% of Americans committed to psychiatric institutions are male. 255

58% of American men usually feel in control of situations they're in. 223

59%

59% of Americans are overweight. 116

59% of American men are happy with the way they look in clothes. 223

59% of Americans aged 8 to 17 would prefer that, regardless of what she does now, their mother would work outside the home. 246

59% of American black babies are born to unmarried mothers. 112

59% of Americans like country music. 236

59% of Americans think doctors do too many tests because of the fear of malpractice suits. 175

59% of Americans have been affected, or know someone personally close to them who has been affected, by air or water pollution. 231

59% of American teenage girls argue with their parents about staying out late. 192

59% of Americans think walking in their neighborhood after dark is risky. 113

59% of American workers are paid hourly rates. 112

59% of Americans think labor unions have too much power. 119

59% of Americans think the honesty and ethical standards of car salesmen are low. 111

59% of Americans do not think judges should use probation for white-collar criminals as an alternative to prison. 210

59% of Americans think the universe is remaining the same size. 254

59% of American suicides shoot themselves. 112

60%

60% of Americans think welfare encourages young women to have babies before marriage. 119

60% of American women think motherhood is the best thing about being a woman. 249

60% of Americans think homosexuals should not be hired as elementary school teachers. 111

60% of Americans do not think schools are giving children discipline. 212

60% of American rapes by a lone assailant are planned. 228

60% of Americans do not spend a lot of time on their personal appearance. 252

60% of Americans do not think that business profits are distributed fairly in America. 119

60% of Americans convicted in US District Court of embezzlement and fraud receive probation. 112

60% of American land owned by the Federal Government is used for forest and wildlife. 112

60% of American teenage girls think all products that pollute the environment should be banned. 202

60% of Americans aged 18 to 25 have tried marijuana at least once in their life. 251

60% of American victims of health care fraud are senior citizens. 282

60% of Americans aged 65 and older are women. 112

61%

61% of Americans aged 13 to 17 think sex education should be taught at home. 246

61% of American wives have seen a pornographic movie. 115

61% of American teenage girls who take photographs most frequently photograph teenagers. 160

61% of American priests believe the public schools are teaching the values of secular humanism. 266

61% of American women have a raincoat. 125

61% of Americans think riding a bicycle is risky. 113

61% of American pocket-pickings occur during the day. 210

61% of American shoppers almost always look over coupons before going to the grocery store. 247

61% of Americans read the daily newspaper. 112

61% of American evening newspapers have a circulation of less than 25,000. 112

61% of Americans strongly believe that smoke detectors in every home should be required by law. 231

61% of Americans who own homeowner's insurance are protected against tornadoes and hurricanes. 231

61% of Americans would be willing to risk the destruction of the United States rather than be dominated by the Soviet Union. 165

61% of Americans do not much like to entertain. 252

62%

62% of American households who consume candy are likely to give candy as a Valentine's Day gift. 191

62% of American wives who are not religious are almost always orgasmic during sex. 115

62% of Americans aged 13 to 17 think you should be 18 or over to decide whether or not to buy pornography. 153

62% of Americans do do-it-yourself projects on a regular basis. 231

62% of American high school seniors like the kind of work they can forget about when the work day is over. 153

62% of Americans aged 8 to 17 think they have the right amount of homework each day. 246

62% of American employees work in companies with fewer than 500 employees. 216

62% of American workers describe their boss as a good listener. 232

62% of American Hispanics socialize with close friends, relatives, or neighbors more than twice a week. 267

62% of Americans think the reason the average tax-payer is honest is because his income is mostly wages and salaries, so he cannot cheat. 244

62% of Americans think a lethal injection is the most humane form of capital punishment. 171

62% of Americans convicted of assault use alcohol just before committing the crime. 250

62% of Americans who earn at least $50,000 a year think the general quality of life in the United States is better now than it was when they were growing up. 212

62% of American households have a frost-free refriger-ator. 112

62% of Americans think a bowel movement each day is necessary for good digestive health. 253

63%

63% of Americans aged 8 to 17 feel good about singing "The Star Spangled Banner." 153

63% of American high school seniors say they would be willing to eat less meat and more grains and vegetables if it would help provide food for starving people. 271

63% of American teenage girls shampoo seven times a week or more. 162

63% of American lawyers think the First Amendment does not prohibit the teaching of creationism in public schools. 140

63% of American 17-year-olds do not know what the Scopes trial was. 207

63% of American women own a cocktail or evening dress. 125

63% of American men do housework on a regular basis. 231

63% of American women return to work within six months of giving birth. 117

63% of American women think power and influence are important in fulfilling their personal goals. 229

63% of American teenage girls think having nice stationery makes letter writing easier and more pleasant. 167

63% of Americans 18 years old and older are married. 112

63% of Americans watch TV almost every evening. 252

63% of American car thefts occur at night. 210

63% of Americans are dissatisfied with the honesty and standards of behavior of people in America today. 110

63% of American wives think marijuana contributes to good sexual experience. 115

63% of Americans who believe in life after death think it will be a paradise of pleasure and delights. 119

64%

64% of American teenage girls think a good return policy is an important factor when they choose a shoe store. 179

64% of American housing units are mortgaged. 112

64% of American hotel and motel rooms are occupied. 112

64% of American teenage girls have hair with split ends. 162

64% of Americans aged 6 to 17 cannot pass a basic fitness test. 117

64% of American teenage girls own a telephone. 248

64% of American working mothers regularly do after-dinner cleanup without help. 197

64% of Americans think welfare encourages husbands to avoid their family responsibilities. 171

64% of Americans think it is important for parents to avoid divorce even if they don't get along. 212

64% of Americans aged 8 to 17 live with both of their natural parents. 246

64% of Americans aged 8 to 17 think there should be busing in the public schools to achieve racial integration. 246

64% of American women aged 19 to 39 would like to lose weight. 111

64% of Americans who own microwave ovens use them only for warming things. 272

64% of Americans strongly believe that government regulation is needed to protect people from dangerous products. 231

64% of American workers drive to work alone. 118

64% of Americans live in the state where they were born. 112

64% of Americans think there are too many foreigners coming to live in the United States these days. 121

64% of American books are softbound. 112

65%

65% of American teenagers who attend evangelical churches say sexual intercourse between unmarried couples is never morally acceptable. 198

65% of Americans like baked beans. 116

65% of American working men say their female coworkers are supportive and helpful. 193

65% of Americans who earn the minimum wage or less are women. 186

65% of American men reject the concept of palimony. 193

65% of Americans think married people are happier than single people. 116

65% of American physicians do not think physicians should be allowed to advertise their professional backgrounds to help consumers decide on a physician. 131

65% of Americans own homeowner's insurance. 231

65% of Americans 16 years old and older participate in the labor force. 112

65% of Americans favor sentencing drunk drivers to jail, even if they have not caused an accident. 210

65% of Americans think drug screening is necessary in certain jobs. 174

65% of Americans make a real effort to eat vegetables like Brussels sprouts and cauliflower. 116

65% of Americans would not object if their employer asked them to take a lie detector test. 210

65% of Americans think God is more like a father figure than a mother figure. 116

65% of American teenage girls use tampons. 161

65% of Americans think that technological developments have an overall positive effect on the environment. 245

65% of American corporate executives think the business community is doing a fair or poor job at preventing the flow of proprietary technology from America to foreign countries. 259

66%

66% of American 19-year-old girls who have never married have had sexual intercourse. 112

66% of American teenage girls send thank-you cards. 167

66% of Americans aged 65 or older who have children live within 30 minutes of one of them. 196

66% of Americans feel young for their age. 117

66% of American men believe in love at first sight. 117

66% of American wives dress in sexually erotic clothing as a stimulus to lovemaking. 115

66% of Americans read the Sunday paper. 112

66% of Americans prefer not to work around people who smoke cigars. 152

66% of American corporate executives think the business community is doing a fair or poor job at cleaning up hazardous wastes. 259

66% of Americans think people get ahead by their own hard work. 151

66% of Americans feel that people with power try to take advantage of people like them. 116

66% of Americans could be killed within 30 days by a large Soviet nuclear attack if people made use of existing shelters near their homes. 233

66% of Americans feel there is life after death. 252

67%

67% of American men mow the lawn on a regular basis. 231

67% of American working mothers regularly do the household vacuuming. 197

67% of Americans aged 13 to 17 believe in angels. 268

67% of Americans believe files are being kept on them for unknown reasons. *117*

67% of Americans have experienced ESP. 269

67% of Americans aged 13 to 17 think that people generally put more pressure on boys than girls to get a good job after they are finished with school. 246

67% of Americans strongly believe that most accidents happen because people are careless or don't pay attention. 231

67% of Americans whose families earn less than $15,000 a year feel they have a good chance of achieving the good life. 153

67% of American widows say they have had contact with the dead. 269

67% of Americans 50 years old and older say they are honest in what they say and do all of the time. 252

67% of American corporate profits are distributed as dividends. 208

67% of Americans think it is common for people on Wall Street to engage in insider trading. 235

67% of Americans think doctors are too interested in making money. 131

67% of Americans favor the death penalty for convicted murderers. 119

67% of Americans think that human nature is basically good. 164

68%

68% of Americans think that God is much more a master than a spouse. 116

68% of Americans do not much like to take chances. 252

68% of American 17-year-olds do not know when the Civil War took place. 207

68% of American parents of students under 18 frequently enforce study hours. 212

68% of American grocery stores have a diet section. 247

68% of Americans do not like others to notice and comment on their appearance. 252

68% of American teenage girls had a permanent in the last year. 162

68% of American veterans aged 55 and older think nursing homes are lonely places to live in. 211

68% of American adults see or talk to their parents at least once a week. 104

68% of Americans often eat beef. 287

68% of American women think contraceptives should be available in high school clinics. 229

68% of Americans feel school officials should be able to search a student's locker at any time. 103

68% of Americans are generally satisfied with their job. 267

68% of Americans favor government financing of projects to create new jobs. 119

68% of Americans think they know how to take advantage of opportunities. 252

68% of American corporate executives think the business community is doing a good or excellent job at paying a fair share of the public tax. 259

68% of Americans think the law should allow doctors to honor the written instructions of their patients, even if that means allowing them to die. 227

68% of Americans arrested for arson are under 18 years of age. 112

68% of American lawyers don't think executions should be open to the public. 146

69%

69% of American cat owners give their pets table scraps. 116

69% of Americans think they should be eating more fish. 274

69% of Americans believe in having as much fun out of life as possible. 116

69% of American drowning deaths involve alcohol. 250

69% of Americans think that if they were too sick to make an important decision about their medical care they would want someone other than their doctor to make it. 227

69% of American high school seniors agree with their parents about whether it's OK to use marijuana. 153

69% of American women who work full-time think day-care centers provide a nurturing environment for children. 229

69% of American public school teachers are women. 199

69% of Americans think adding a little more than they actually paid when reporting business expenses is acceptable. 244

69% of Americans think America is spending too much money on foreign aid. 119

69% of Americans think politics and government sometimes get so complicated that they can't really understand what's going on. 153

69% of Americans who own a firearm say that if a burglar broke into their home at night they would use it. 210

69% of Americans do not take the lead in talking with people. 252

70%

70% of American men who earn $70,000 a year or more cheat on their wives. 117

70% of Americans are very likely to donate a loved one's organs. 117

70% of American personnel administrators think there is nothing an organization can do to stop workplace romances. 273

70% of Americans think homosexuality is morally wrong. 152

70% of American chief executives of large companies think that American industry is too focused on the short term. 243

70% of Americans think the government does not know how to eliminate poverty even if it were willing to spend whatever necessary. 153

70% of American purse snatchings occur during the day. 210

70% of American fathers win child-custody cases they contest. 117

70% of American women under the age of 30 want a family and a career. 193

70% of American independent pet stores sell fish food. 156

70% of American lawyers think bar exams do not measure ability to practice law. 140

70% of American men arrested for serious crimes in major cities have illicit drugs in their bodies. 188

70% of Americans who report to a supervisor at work would be comfortable discussing coughing up blood with him. 253

70% of American single-vehicle traffic fatalities that occur on a weekend night involve an intoxicated driver. 250

70% of American murders lead to the arrest of a suspect. 101

70% of American teenage girls use lip gloss. 173

70% of Americans own running shoes but don't run. *117*

70% of Americans aged 30 and older do not pay attention to cholesterol in their diet. 120

70% of Americans like meat loaf. 116

70% of Americans who go to a chiropractor for relief of physical pain meet with success. 267

70% of Americans believe Jesus is God. 269

71%

71% of Americans who have been divorced say they are happier than they were before the divorce. 109

71% of American men think women should call men for a date. 193

71% of American physicians believe medical costs can be reduced without reducing the quality of care. 131

71% of American high school seniors prefer to date people who don't smoke. 271

71% of Americans are members of a church or synagogue. 112

71% of Americans think the Arabs are determined to destroy Israel. 239

71% of American smokers have tried to quit. 119

72%

72% of American colleges and universities allow students to graduate without studying American history or literature. 209

72% of Americans think that to improve the quality of education in American schools it is important to provide more sports and fitness programs. 212

72% of American babies often eat vegetables. 287

72% of American workers say their boss is fair. 232

72% of Americans prefer not to work around people who have AIDS. 152

72% of American violent crime against whites is committed by whites. 194

72% of American teenage girls use face powder. 173

72% of American Yuppies think that Yuppies are more concerned with their own needs than with other people's. 116

72% of Americans discharged from nursing homes are alive. 133

72% of American shoppers feel the express checkout in their supermarket is good or excellent. 257

72% of Americans would be more likely to buy American than foreign shoes. 262

72% of Americans have flown in a commercial airplane. 218

**72% of American females find shopping
a pleasant experience.** 252

72% of American adults would choose their in-laws for friends even if they were not related. 104

72% of American women think women can have a happy and complete life without getting married. 193

72% of American wives who are very religious are almost always orgasmic during sex. 115

73%

73% of American teenage girls have dated a boy of another religion. 192

73% of Americans aged 13 to 17 think that people need be no more than 18 before they make their own decisions about having sex. 246

73% of Americans have had a headache in the last year. 267

73% of American high school students attend schools with at least 700 students. 112

73% of American households have a washing machine. 112

73% of American women think there should be a federal law guaranteeing paternity leave. 229

73% of Americans aged 18 to 36 think children should be sure their elderly parents are not lonely. 201

73% of Americans prefer not to work around people who use foul language. *152*

74%

74% of Americans think taking the law into one's hands is sometimes justified. 114

74% of Americans disapprove of wiretapping. 210

74% of American murder victims are male. 210

74% of American teenage girls do not intend to keep their names when they marry. 192

74% of American adults have a high school diploma. 150

74% of Americans say that if they had their life to live over they would continue with their formal education. 252

74% of Americans think science and technology may destroy the human race. 117

75%

75% of Americans could be killed within 30 days by a large Soviet nuclear attack if no civil defense measures were taken. 233

75% of American grocery stores have a magazine reading center. 247

75% of American rapes of blacks are committed by blacks. 210

75% of Americans over 65 years of age think extra vitamins provide more pep and energy. 282

75% of Americans who are unemployed receive no unemployment benefits. 117

75% of Americans, if given enough money to live comfortably for the rest of their lives, would still keep working. 151

75% of Americans think most advertising seeks to per-
suade people to buy things they don't need or
can't afford. 261

75% of American ministers favor the use of public
schools for after-hours religious activities. 266

75% of American women think that men should get
married at age 25 or older. 193

75% of American women often think of their physical
appearance. 116

75% of American women wear the wrong size bras. 117

75% of American hunters go for big game. 112

76%

76% of American wives vary locations or settings for sex to make it more exciting. 115

76% of Americans have tried cigarettes. 251

76% of Americans are concerned about threats to their personal privacy. 119

76% of Americans aged 18 to 44 say they had little to do with the protests and controversies of the 1960s and early 1970s. 222

76% of Americans think congressional candidates make promises they have no intention of fulfilling. 114

76% of Americans think the bad effects of alcoholic beverages outweigh the good. 113

76% of American shoppers think residues in food, such as pesticides and herbicides, are a serious hazard. 257

76% of Americans think the government wastes a lot of the money we pay in taxes. 157

76% of Americans feel hostile toward the Soviet Union. 238

76% of American owners of small businesses do not have a college degree. 265

76% of Americans think we should have import quotas to limit foreign products coming into the country. 121

76% of Americans would be more likely to buy an American than a foreign car. 262

77%

77% of Americans live in metropolitan areas. 112

77% of American fathers say their sex life suffers after they and their partners have children. 276

77% of American rapes are committed without a weapon. 194

77% of Americans aged 8 to 17 like school. 246

77% of Americans who own stock finished at least one year of college. 225

77% of Americans think most poor people have been poor for a long time and will probably remain poor. 171

77% of Americans think the TV evangelical movement has made a mockery of what religion should be. 242

77% of American working mothers regularly prepare the household dinner without help. 197

77% of Americans have never had the desire to hold a position in government. 252

77% of American corporate executives think the business community is doing a good or excellent job at ensuring product safety. 259

77% of American shoppers think artificial coloring in food is a hazard. 257

77% of Americans are satisfied with their lives. 252

77% of American suicides are male. 112

78%

78% of Americans think many hostile takeovers are engineered by groups of big investors who are trying to drive up the price of the stock just to make a profit for themselves. 230

78% of Americans think most people would take an illegal insider tip and buy stock to make money. 235

78% of Americans are satisfied with their financial situation. 151

78% of American 17-year-old girls do not know that Betty Friedan and Gloria Steinem were leaders of the women's movement of the 1970s. 207

78% of American college students go to public colleges. 112

78% of American females aged 15 to 21 have a driver's license. 181

78% of American physicians conduct some tests only because of the threat of malpractice suits. 175

78% of American women think there are substantial risks involved in using birth control pills. 113

78% of Americans often eat potatoes. 287

78% of Americans have not contributed money to a political party or candidate in the last four years. 119

78% of American corporate executives think the business community is doing a fair or poor job at retraining workers whose skills are obsolete. 259

78% of Americans think that refugees entering the country are an important threat to America. 121

78% of Americans think they have a good chance of achieving the good life. 153

79%

79% of American fathers are in the delivery room when their children are born. 117

79% of American leading central nervous system scientists think that by the year 2000 the transplant of fetal brain tissue into the human brain will be acceptable. 218

79% of Americans aged 8 to 17 are happy with the amount of time their parents spend with them. 246

79% of Americans who have children in their households have had a headache in the last year. 267

79% of American adults are missing at least one tooth. 163

79% of American grits-eaters eat a cup or less at a sitting. 288

79% of American families have a checking account. 112

79% of Americans think bad work attitudes in America are an important reason the US is not competitive in world trade. 260

79% of Americans with children in the home hope the children become God-fearing, strictly moral people. 283

79% of Americans with children in the home hope the children will grow up to make a lot of money. 283

80%

***80%** of American dog owners give their pets table scraps.* 116

80% of Americans do not discuss fees up front with their doctor. 131

80% of Americans favor blood tests for AIDS for people applying for marriage licenses. 285

80% of American high school seniors think that if they cheated on a test their peers would not care. 271

80% of American blacks think that if an equally qualified white and black are competing for a job, the black is less likely to be hired. 281

80% of Americans have not had their opinion about the ethics of the people who work on Wall Street change much because of the stories of insider trading. 237

80% of American teenage girls play Monopoly. 177

80% of American high school seniors think people should do their own thing, even if other people think it's strange. 271

81%

81% of American teenage girls choose their own brand of deodorant. 161

81% of American high school seniors are, on the whole, satisfied with themselves. 153

81% of American abortions are performed on unmarried women. 112

81% of American physicians think that if a dying patient in severe distress which cannot be relieved asks to have his life ended, it is not ethically permissible to comply. 227

81% of American violent crime against blacks is committed by blacks. 194

81% of American jail inmates who are convicted plead guilty. 112

81% of directors of large American corporations do not think Congress should protect American business from foreign competition. 132

81% of Americans believe the rich get richer and the poor get poorer. 116

81% of American Yuppies think that Yuppies are inclined to buy showy clothes and cars to set themselves apart from other people. 116

81% of Americans often drink milk. 287

81% of American widowed, divorced, or separated women think marriage is a commitment for life. 229

82%

82% of American adults watch prime-time television. 112

82% of American mothers say their sex life suffers after they and their partners have children. 276

82% of American entertainment celebrities watch their own performances on film or TV. 130

82% of Americans are satisfied with their work. 151

82% of unemployed Americans are generally satisfied with their life. 267

82% of American teenagers say that homework makes them anxious. 117

82% of American shoppers frequently make a list before going to the grocery store. 247

82% of American Navy officers tried in Courts-Martial are convicted. 210

82% of American enlisted personnel are given an honorable discharge. 112

82% of American visitors from overseas have been here before. 213

82% of American residents who were born in Mexico are not citizens. 112

82% of Americans do not feel that they will ever see total peace between all nations in their lifetime. 252

83%

83% of Americans feel close to God. 119

83% of Americans are not much bothered by getting older. 252

83% of Americans who go to a spiritual counselor or faith healer for relief of physical pain meet with success. 267

83% of American 17-year-old blacks do not know when Lincoln was president. 207

83% of American rapes of whites are committed by whites. 210

83% of Americans who earn the minimum wage or less are white. 186

83% of American companies have fewer than 20 employees.

83% of American women think we need more sex education in the schools. 229

83% of American cashiers are women. 112

83% of American lawyers think smokers should bear the responsibility for the consequences of smoking. 142

83% of American teenage girls brush their teeth at least twice a day. 161

83% of Americans who are arrested are male. 112

83% of Americans do not like to be the center of attention. 252

83% of Americans held up by a robber with a gun are not injured. 194

83% of Americans think a nuclear power plant could explode like a bomb. 147

83% of Americans think love is the primary reason people get married. 193

83% of American parents with children under 18 sit and talk with their children daily. 212

83% of Americans think it is sometimes necessary to discipline a child with a good, hard spanking. 119

83% of American adults would choose their parents for friends even if they were not related. 104

83% of American high school seniors think people are at great risk of harming themselves if they take LSD regularly. 210

83% of Americans think drug abuse will never be stopped because many Americans will be willing to pay lots of money for drugs. 210

84%

84% of American inmates of state prisons live in housing units of less than 40 square feet. 210

84% of Americans think the courts do not deal harshly enough with criminals. 150

84% of Americans with children in the home hope the children learn to walk the straight and narrow. 283

84% of American men think a father's role in raising children is just as important as the mother's. 223

84% of American teenage girls use lipstick. 173

84% of American girls aged 8 to 17 are very concerned about kidnapping. 246

84% of American physicians say they would be likely to administer pain-relieving drugs to a dying patient in severe distress even if they might shorten the patient's life. 227

84% of Americans believe heaven exists. 117

84% of Americans own auto insurance. 231

84% of American women aged 45 to 64 are married. 112

84% of Americans say they would not oppose a marriage between a family member and a person with a severe physical handicap. 152

84% of American grocery stores offer carry-out services. 247

84% of Americans who use a video display terminal have had a headache in the last year. 267

84% of Americans think welfare makes people work less than they would if there wasn't a welfare system. 119

84% of Americans who earn less than $15,000 a year consider themselves happy people. 252

85%

85% of American high school seniors expect that if they get married they will stay with the same person for life. 153

85% of Americans would remarry their spouse if they had it to do over again. 252

85% of Americans who are college-educated can imagine a situation in which they would approve of a policeman's striking a man. 210

85% of Americans do not think they understand the meaning of monoclonal antibodies. 245

85% of Americans think it is important to have one parent not working until the children are in school. 212

85% of Americans aged 8 to 17 feel good about the clothes they wear. 246

85% of Americans arrested for gambling are male. 210

85% of American migrant farmworkers are male. 278

85% of Americans believe a terminally ill patient sustained by life-support machines has the right to tell the doctor to pull the plug. 116

85% of Americans who believe in life after death think it will be a place of loving intellectual communion. 119

85% of Americans consider themselves somewhat or very religious. 252

85% of Americans did not see Halley's comet. 110

85% of Americans who own stock live in metropolitan areas. 225

85% of American shoppers think sugar in food is a hazard. 257

85% of the alcoholic beverages Americans drink is beer. 112

85% of Americans who buy a new American car buy one with air conditioning. 256

85% of Americans think that, all in all, one can live well in America. 119

86%

86% of American entertainment celebrities think entertainers are influential in shaping public taste. 130

86% of American leading central nervous system scientists think that by the year 2000 traditional psychoanalytic therapy will be unimportant. 218

86% of American assaults are committed by men. 210

86% of American men use deodorant. 117

86% of American teenage girls ate in a fast-food restaurant last week. 248

86% of American colleges and universities allow students to graduate without studying classical Greece and Rome. 209

86% of American lawyers who advertise use the Yellow Pages. 138

86% of American senior citizens think crime has gotten worse since they were growing up. 212

86% of American single women think there should be a federal law guaranteeing paternity leave. 229

86% of American high school seniors think marijuana or hashish is easy to come by. 210

86% of Americans like mashed potatoes. 116

86% of American employees of medium and large firms are given free parking at work. 112

86% of American high school seniors think taking heroin in public places should be illegal. 210

86% of Americans with children under 18 are optimistic about their children's future. 212

87%

87% of American women do not think it is acceptable to have extramarital sex. 229

87% of Americans aged 13 to 17 think that people should be at least 18 before they decide about getting married. 246

87% of Americans expect special problems with marriages between blacks and whites. 119

87% of Americans with children in the home hope the children will want to work for an end to discrimination against women and racial minorities. 283

87% of American lead air pollution is produced by motor vehicles. 112

87% of Americans arrested for offenses against family and children are male. 210

87% of American physicians are male. 112

87% of American physicians do not make house calls to private homes. 131

87% of American 5-year-olds are enrolled in school. 112

87% of American high school districts do not require competency tests for teachers. 112

87% of American librarians are women. 112

87% of American women are less than 5′6″ tall. 279

87% of Americans prefer not to work around people who don't use deodorant. 152

87% of American hunters go for small game. 112

88%

88% of Americans aged 8 to 17 feel good about what their parents do for a living. 153

88% of American women say that if they could afford it they would rather stay home with their children. 229

88% of American households have at least one member who eats candy. 191

88% of American teenage girls use perfume. 169

88% of Americans think government must keep a sharp eye on business to get it to clean up its own air and water pollution. 157

88% of American women think there should be more restrictions of pornographic material. 229

88% of American teenage girls bathe seven or more times a week. 169

89%

89% of American chief executives of large companies think that responding to a hostile takeover bid is stressful. 243

89% of American companies do not provide child-care assistance to employees. 197

89% of American children in one-parent households live with their mother. 185

89% of American single women think it is acceptable for a woman who has never been married to have and raise children by herself. 229

89% of American women think there should be a federal law guaranteeing maternity leave. 229

89% of American grocery stores sell motor oil. 247

89% of American high school seniors have had an argument or fight with their parents in the last year. 210

89% of Americans aged 50 and over do not often wish they were teenagers again. 252

89% of American fishermen fish in fresh water. 112

89% of Americans who die are embalmed and put in a casket. 148

89% of Americans are very proud to be American. 110

90%

90% of American refrigerators are white or almond. 117

90% of American public school principals are white. 199

90% of American vandals are male. 101

90% of American information clerks are female. 112

90% of American teenage girls own jewelry. 248

90% of American group rapes are planned. 228

90% of Americans consider themselves happy people. 252

90% of American men drive on a regular basis. 231

90% of Americans think driving a car is risky. 113

90% of American young adults have used alcohol in the last year. 210

90% of Americans think it is important for parents to use strict discipline with children. 212

90% of American married women say they do most of the cooking in the household. 272

90% of American women think it takes just as much drive and intelligence to raise children properly as it does to hold a good position in business or government. 193

90% of American beer drinkers drink three beers or less per sitting. 288

90% of American Indian homicides are alcohol-related. 250

90% of Americans who believe in life after death think it will be a reunion with loved ones. 119

90% of Americans with children in the home think the children inherited their parents' good looks. 283

91%

91% of married Americans think playing a musical instrument is something you'll always be glad you learned to do. 195

91% of American teenage girls think the right greeting card can express feelings that are hard to say in person or on the telephone. 167

91% of American teenage girls use nail polish. 173

91% of American chefs and restaurant owners feel the use of daily specials matters to their customers. 127

91% of Americans aged 8 to 17 are happy with the size of their family. 246

91% of American teenage girls think the ideal age for marriage is 25 or younger. 192

91% of American churches are Protestant. 112

91% of American women have confidence in doctors. 229

91% of American airline passengers use discount fares. 217

92%

92% of Americans who would be troubled if the universe were expanding feel that way because there might then be danger to the earth. 254

92% of American women have confidence in scientists. 229

92% of Americans aged 8 to 17 feel their family and home life is happy. 153

92% of American households have telephone service. 112

92% of American veterans aged 55 and older think it's better to stay out of nursing homes as long as you can. 211

92% of American Air Force enlisted personnel tried in Courts-Martial are convicted. 210

92% of American employees of medium and large firms get paid leave for jury duty. 112

92% of American women use deodorant. 117

92% of American burglars are male. 101

92% of Americans prefer not to work around people who get high during the day. 152

92% of American physicians favor setting a limit on pain-and-suffering awards in medical malpractice cases. 175

92% *of American shoppers think salt in food is a hazard.* 257

92% of Americans think poverty will always be a major problem for our society. 171

92% of American corporations have business receipts of at least one million dollars. 112

93%

93% of Americans aged 8 to 17 are happy about the amount of love their parents show them. 246

93% of Americans think it is very important for parents to spend more time with children. 212

93% of Americans think gambling is risky. *113*

93% of American women think health care and related services in this country are too expensive. 229

93% of American bank tellers are women. 112

93% of American women think religion is important in fulfilling their personal goals. 229

93% of American companies have fewer than 100 employees. 216

93% of Americans think that to improve the quality of education in American schools it is important not to pass poor students to the next grade. 212

93% of new American transportation toys cannot be ridden on. 135

93% of Americans say they have never overstated their tax deductions, even by just a small amount. 244

93% of Americans arrested by the US Secret Service are convicted. 210

93% of American teenage girls who bake desserts put frosting on them. 172

94%

94% of American parents of children under 18 say their children have never run away from home overnight or longer. 212

94% of Americans with children in the home hope the children go on to do things they never did. 283

94% of American women do housework on a regular basis. 231

94% of American backyard gardeners grow tomatoes. 117

94% of American women change their health habits on the advice of their physicians when they become pregnant. 116

94% of American teenage girls talked on the phone last week.

94% of Americans want their doctor to tell them everything about their medical condition, even if it is unfavorable. 227

94% of American chefs and restaurant owners are satisfied with how well-mannered their customers are. 127

94% of American dietitians are female. 112

94% of American pancake eaters eat more than one a sitting. 288

94% of American deportable aliens who are located come from Mexico. 112

94% of American men would change something about their looks if they could. 116

95%

95% of American unskilled laborers are generally satisfied with their life. 267

95% of American high school seniors think having lots of money is important in their life. 271

95% of Americans whose families earn at least $40,000 a year are happy with things these days. 153

95% of American parents of children under 18 say their girls have never been pregnant. 212

95% of American teenage girls plan to marry. 192

95% of American registered nurses are female. 112

95% of Americans aged 8 to 17 have at least one living grandparent. 246

95% of Americans think it is an important obligation of citizenship to keep fully informed about news and public issues. 164

95% of Americans who buy a new American car buy one with power steering. 256

95% of Americans believe in God. 116

95% of American cocaine users snort it. 251

95% of American households do not purchase dehydrated potatoes. 284

95% of American peanut eaters eat at least nine at a sitting. 288

96%

96% of American state prison inmates are male. 194

96% of American school superintendents are men. 199

96% of American law enforcement officers who are killed are men. 210

96% of American parents of children under 18 say their children have never had problems with the law. 212

96% of American wives have not engaged in sexual mate-swapping. 115

96% of Americans think that everyone who buys a home or auto should insure it. 231

96% of American Yuppies consider themselves happy people. 252

96% of American schoolchildren can identify Ronald McDonald (who is second only to Santa Claus). 187

97%

97% of American women think having and raising a family is important in fulfilling their personal goals. 229

97% of American abortions are done by curettage. 102

97% of American households do not purchase baby food. 284

97% of American teenage girls use eye make-up. 173

97% of American teenage girls have had a skin problem in the last month. 159

97% of Americans think their spouses are honest with them about anything really important most or all of the time. 114

97% of American grocery stores offer paper bags. 247

97% of Americans think smoking is risky. 113

97% of American wives have not, since the age of 18, had sex with a woman. 115

98%

98% of American women think self-growth is important in fulfilling their personal goals. 229

98% of Americans often eat vegetables. 287

98% of American secretaries are women. 112

98% of Americans think it is an important obligation of citizenship to be able to speak and understand English. 164

98% of American households have at least one television. 112

98% of Americans think smoking in bed is risky. 113

98% of Americans think it is an important obligation of citizenship for young men to serve in the military when the country is at war. 164

98% of American Marine Corps officers tried in Courts-Martial are convicted. 210

98% of American high school seniors do not think they will be taking LSD in five years. 271

98% of American multiple births are twins. 221

99%

99% of American kindergarten teachers are women. 112

99% of American rapists are male. 101

99% of American dental assistants are women. 112

99% of American firefighters are men. 112

99% of Americans think it is an important obligation of citizenship to report a crime a citizen has witnessed. 164

99% of American employees of medium and large firms get paid vacations. 112

99% of American households have at least one radio. 112

99% of American automobile mechanics are men. 112

99% of American teenage girls use a deodorant. 161

99% of American women would change something about their looks if they could. 116

99% of American women think contributing to or bettering society is important in fulfilling their personal goals. 229

100%

100% of Americans are, if nothing else, Americans.

Appendix

101. *Uniform Crime Reports: Crime in the United States—1986.* Federal Bureau of Investigation. US Department of Justice.
102. *Health United States 1986.* Public Health Service. US Department of Health and Human Services.
103. *Parents* Magazine. January 1988.
104. *Parents* Magazine. December 1987.
105. *Parents* Magazine. October 1987.
106. *Parents* Magazine. September 1987.
107. *Parents* Magazine. June 1987.
108. *Parents* Magazine. May 1987.
109. *Parents* Magazine. January 1987.
110. *The Gallup Poll—Public Opinion 1986.* George Gallup, Jr. Scholarly Resources, Inc.
111. *The Gallup Poll—Public Opinion 1985.* George Gallup, Jr. Scholarly Resources, Inc.
112. *Statistical Abstract of the United States 1987.* Bureau of the Census. US Department of Commerce.
113. *Public Opinion.* February/March 1986.
114. *Public Opinion.* November/December 1986.
115. *The Redbook Report on Female Sexuality.* Carol Tavris and Susan Sadd. Delacorte. 1977.
116. *Inside America.* Louis Harris. Vintage. 1987.
117. *The Harper's Index.* Lewis Lapham, Michael Pollan, Eric Etheridge. Henry Holt. 1987.
118. *1980 Census of Population: General Social and Economic Characteristics, United States Summary.* Bureau of the Census. US Department of Commerce. 1983.
119. *General Social Surveys, 1972–1987.* Conducted for The National Data Program for the Social Sciences at National Opinion Research Center, University of Chicago.
120. *The New York Times.* January 6, 1988.
121. "A Survey of Public Attitudes Toward Refugees and Immi-

grants." Kane, Parsons, and Associates, Inc. 1984. Proprietary study submitted to United States Committee for Refugees.

122. "Women's Place: Attitudes of Young American Women Toward Feminism and Related Issues." Kane, Parsons, and Associates, Inc. 1982. Proprietary study submitted to *Parents* Magazine.

123. *Clothes.* January 1, 1978.

124. *Apparel Merchandising.* July 1986.

125. Fairchild Fact File: "The Customer Speaks About Her Wardrobe." Fairchild Publications. 1978.

126. "A Survey of Local Television News Anchorpersons." Kane, Parsons, and Associates, Inc. 1981. Proprietary study submitted to Rowland Company.

127. "Taste in America: Chefs and Restaurant Proprietors." Kane, Parsons, and Associates, Inc. 1984. Proprietary study prepared for Popeye's Famous Fried Chicken.

128. Popeye's "Spice in Your Life" Series. Kane, Parsons, and Associates, Inc. 1983. Proprietary study submitted to Popeye's Famous Fried Chicken.

129. *American Bar Association Journal.* Dan Bowdren Associates. December 1, 1986.

130. "A Survey of Attitudes, Perceptions, and Experiences Among Entertainment Celebrities." Kane, Parsons, and Associates, Inc. 1983. Proprietary study submitted to Popeye's Famous Fried Chicken.

131. *Physician and Public Attitudes on Health Care Issues.* Larry Freshnock. American Medical Association. 1984.

132. *Issues Facing US Corporate Directors.* Touche Ross International. 1986.

133. *Advancedata.* Vital and Health Statistics. US Department of Health and Human Services. September 30, 1987.

134. *Current Estimates from the National Health Interview Survey.* Vital and Health Statistics. Public Health Service. US Department of Health and Human Services. 1987.

135. *Toy Industry Fact Book.* Toy Manufacturers of America. 1987.

136. *Annual Energy Review 1986.* Energy Information Administration.

137. *The Attitudes of Science Policy, Environmental, and Utility Leaders on US Energy Issues and Fusion.* J.D. Miller, Lawrence Livermore National Laboratory. 1986.

138. *American Bar Association Journal.* Kane, Parsons, and Associates, Inc. November 1, 1987.

139. *American Bar Association Journal.* Kane, Parsons, and Associates, Inc. September 1, 1987.
140. *American Bar Association Journal.* Kane, Parsons, and Associates, Inc. July 1, 1987.
141. *American Bar Association Journal.* Kane, Parsons, and Associates, Inc. January 1, 1987.
142. *American Bar Association Journal.* Dan Bowdren Associates. October 1, 1986.
143. *American Bar Association Journal.* Dan Bowdren Associates. September 1, 1986.
144. *American Bar Association Journal.* Kane, Parsons, and Associates, Inc. June 1, 1986.
145. *American Bar Association Journal.* Kane, Parsons, and Associates, Inc. November 1, 1985.
146. *American Bar Association Journal.* Kane, Parsons, and Associates, Inc. April 1, 1985.
147. *Public Opinion.* February/March 1984.
148. Casket Manufacturer's Association.
149. A Survey of Women Officers of America's Largest Corporations. Kane, Parsons, and Associates, Inc. 1982. Proprietary study submitted to Rowland Company.
150. *Public Opinion.* November/December 1987.
151. *Public Opinion.* September/October 1987.
152. *Public Opinion.* July/August 1987.
153. *Public Opinion.* May/June 1987.
154. Pet Food Institute Fact Sheet 1986.
155. *The Pet Dealer.* December 1987.
156. "The 1986 Sales/Profit Picture: Independent Pet Retailers." Pets Supplies Marketing.
157. *Public Opinion.* March/April 1987.
158. *Public Opinion.* January/February 1987.
159. Skin Care Survey. *Seventeen* Magazine. 1985.
160. Photography Survey. *Seventeen* Magazine. 1986.
161. Personal Hygiene Survey. *Seventeen* Magazine. 1985.
162. Hair Care Survey. *Seventeen* Magazine. 1985.
163. *Decayed, Missing, and Filled Teeth Among Persons 1–74 Years.* Vital and Health Statistics. US Department of Health and Human Services. 1981.
164. *Public Opinion.* October/November 1986.
165. *Public Opinion.* Summer 1986.

166. Special Study of Moisturizer Usage. *Seventeen* Magazine. 1985.
167. Greeting Card Purchasing Habits and Letter Writing Patterns Among Teen Girls. *Seventeen* Magazine. 1983.
168. *Public Opinion.* August/September 1985.
169. Fragrance Survey. *Seventeen* Magazine. 1985.
170. Fragrance Omnibus. *Seventeen* Magazine. 1985.
171. *Public Opinion.* June/July 1985.
172. Food Survey. *Seventeen* Magazine. 1986.
173. Cosmetic Survey. *Seventeen* Magazine. 1986.
174. *American Medical Association Surveys of Physician and Public Opinion on Health Care Issues.* 1987.
175. *American Medical Association Surveys of Physician and Public Opinion.* 1986.
176. Class Ring Survey. *Seventeen* Magazine. 1987.
177. Board/Card/VCR Game Survey. *Seventeen* Magazine. 1986.
178. *Maternal Weight Gain and the Outcome of Pregnancy.* Vital and Health Statistics. US Department of Health and Human Services. 1986.
179. Footwear Survey. *Seventeen* Magazine. 1984.
180. Statistical Record. Cigar Association of America, Inc. 1988.
181. Automotive Survey. *Seventeen* Magazine. 1987.
182. *Percutaneous Immediate Hypersensitivity to Eight Allergens.* Vital and Health Statistics. US Department of Health and Human Services. 1986.
183. *Arts and Sciences Newsletter.* Cornell University. Fall 1987.
184. "Sports and Mass Media." *Gannett Center Journal.* Fall 1987.
185. *The New York Times.* January 28, 1988.
186. *The New York Times.* January 24, 1988.
187. "Fascinating McFacts." McDonald's Corporation. 1984.
188. *The New York Times.* January 22, 1988.
189. *The Economist.* January 9, 1988.
190. 1985–1986 Annual Report: US Pharmaceutical Industry. Pharmaceutical Manufacturers Association.
191. News. National Confectioners Association.
192. The Teen Girl of 1984. *Seventeen* Magazine. 1984.
193. The 1985 Virginia Slims American Women's Opinion Poll. The Roper Organization, Inc. 1985.
194. *Report to the Nation on Crime and Justice.* US Department of Justice. 1983.
195. *"Music USA 87"—1987 Review of the Music Industry and Adult*

Attitudes Toward Music Survey. American Music Conference.
196. "A Profile of Older Americans: 1987." American Association of Retired Persons.
197. *New York Newsday.* February 2, 1988.
198. *New York Newsday.* February 2, 1988.
199. *The New York Times.* January 20, 1988.
200. "First Marriage Brides, According to Age." Research from *Seventeen.* US Department of Health and Human Services. Vital Statistics Report. 1983.
201. *Public Opinion.* April/May 1985.
202. "Opinions on Current Issues, Female Teens 12–19." Research from *Seventeen.* Simmons Teen Age Research Studies. 1986.
203. Society of American Florists Floral Marketing Report. 1985.
204. 1987 Rand Youth Poll. Youth Research Institute.
205. *Gaming and Wagering Business.* July 1987.
206. *Update.* Alcohol, Drug Abuse, and Mental Health Administration. US Department of Health and Human Services. Fall 1987.
207. *What Do Our 17-Year-Olds Know?* Diane Ravitch, Chester Finn, Jr. Harper and Row. 1987.
208. *Country Report: USA.* Fourth Quarter 1987. The Economist Intelligence Unit.
209. "To Reclaim a Legacy." Secretary of Education William J. Bennett. National Endowment of the Humanities. 1984.
210. *Sourcebook of Criminal Justice Statistics—1986.* US Department of Justice.
211. "Survey of Aging Veterans: A Study of the Means, Resources, and Future Expectations of Veterans Aged 55 and Over." Louis Harris and Associates, Inc. 1985. Conducted for the Veterans Administration.
212. "Children's Needs and Public Responsibilities: A Survey of American Attitudes About the Problems and Prospects of American Children." Louis Harris and Associates, Inc. 1986. Conducted for Group W—Westinghouse Broadcasting Co.
213. *Travel Industry World Yearbook: The Big Picture—1987.* Somerset Waters. Child and Waters, Inc.
214. 1987 Nielsen Report on Television. Nielsen Media Research.
215. *The Economist.* March 26, 1988.
216. *The Economist.* March 5, 1988.
217. *The New York Times.* March 20, 1988.
218. "The Bristol-Myers Report: Medicine in the Next Century."

Louis Harris and Associates, Inc. 1987.

219. *The Statistical Bulletin.* Metropolitan Life Insurance Company. October-December 1986.

220. *The Statistical Bulletin.* Metropolitan Life Insurance Company. October-December 1987.

221. *The Statistical Bulletin.* Metropolitan Life Insurance Company. January-March 1988.

222. *Rolling Stone.* April 7, 1988.

223. "The American Male Opinion Index." *Gentlemen's Quarterly.* 1988.

224. *Hypertension in Adults.* Vital and Health Statistics. US Department of Health and Human Services. 1981.

225. Shareownership 1985. New York Stock Exchange, Inc.

226. "Survey of Female Veterans: A Study of the Needs, Attitudes, and Experiences of Women Veterans." Louis Harris and Associates, Inc. 1985. Conducted for the Veterans Administration.

227. "Making Health Care Decisions: The Ethical and Legal Implications of Informed Consent in the Patient-Practitioner Relationship." President's Commission for the Study of Ethical Problems in Medicine and Biomedical and Behavioral Research. 1982.

228. U. The National College Newspaper.

229. "Annual Study of Women's Attitudes." Mark Clements Research, Inc. 1987.

230. "A Study of the Attitudes of the American People and Top Business Executives Toward Hostile Corporate Takeovers." Louis Harris and Associates, Inc. Conducted for the Institute of Private Enterprise at the University of North Carolina. 1987.

231. "Public Attitudes Toward Risk." Louis Harris and Associates, Inc. Conducted for The Insurance Information Institute. 1983.

232. *New York Newsday.* February 9, 1988.

233. *The Effects of Nuclear War.* Office of Technology Assessment. Congress of the United States. 1979.

234. Business Week/Harris Poll. August 25, 1986.

235. Business Week/Harris Poll. December 8, 1986.

236. The Harris Survey. February 24, 1986.

237. The Harris Survey. March 23, 1987.

238. The Harris Survey. March 16, 1987.

239. The Harris Survey. March 30, 1987.

240. The Harris Survey. December 28, 1987.

241. Business Week/Harris Poll. July 20, 1987.

242. The Harris Survey. April 20, 1987.
243. Business Week/Harris Poll. October 23, 1987.
244. *Public Opinion.* February/March 1985.
245. "Public Attitudes Toward Science, Biotechnology, and Genetic Engineering." Louis Harris and Associates, Inc. Submitted to the Office of Technology Assessment. 1987.
246. The American Chicle Youth Poll. The Roper Organization, Inc. Commissioned by The American Chicle Group, Warner-Lambert Company. 1987.
247. *Progressive Grocer.* April 1987.
248. Teenage Research Unlimited. Fall 1987.
249. *New York Newsday.* February 16, 1988.
250. "Sixth Special Report to the US Congress on Alcohol and Health." From the Secretary of Health and Human Services. January 1987.
251. "NIDA Capsules." National Institute on Drug Abuse. November 1986.
252. "America in the Eighties." RH Bruskin Associates Market Research. 1985.
253. "A National Survey of Public Perceptions of Digestive Health and Disease: Lack of Knowledge, Misinformation, and Myth." National Digestive Disease Education Program. 1984.
254. "Contemporary Cosmological Beliefs." Alan Lightman, Jon Miller, Bonnie Leadbeater. *Social Studies of Science.* 1987.
255. "Mental Health, United States, 1987." Alcohol, Drug Abuse, and Mental Health Administration. US Department of Health and Human Services.
256. "% '87 Model US Car Factory-Installed Equipment." Ward's Automotive Reports. 1988.
257. "Trends Update: 1987 Consumer Attitudes and the Supermarket." Food Marketing Institute.
258. ORC Issue Watch. Opinion Research Corporation. November 1987.
259. ORC Issue Watch. Opinion Research Corporation. October 1987.
260. ORC Issue Watch. Opinion Research Corporation. September 1987.
261. ORC Issue Watch. Opinion Research Corporation. August 1987.
262. ORC Issue Watch. Opinion Research Corporation. July 1987.

263. ORC Issue Watch. Opinion Research Corporation. June 1986.

264. ORC Issue Watch. Opinion Research Corporation. February 1986.

265. *Business Week.* February 8, 1988.

266. *Jewish Exponent.* February 12, 1988.

267. "The Nuprin Pain Report." Louis Harris and Associates, Inc. Bristol-Myers Products. 1985.

268. The Gallup Youth Poll. October 29, 1986.

269. *American Health.* January/February 1987.

270. *The Skeptical Inquirer,* Vol. 10. Summer 1986.

271. *Monitoring the Future: Questionnaire Responses from the Nation's High School Seniors.* Jerald Bachman, Lloyd Johnston, Patrick O'Malley. Institute for Social Research, The University of Michigan. 1986.

272. *The New York Times.* February 24, 1988.

273. *The Boston Herald.* February 12, 1988.

274. *Parents* Magazine. April 1988.

275. *Parents* Magazine. May 1988.

276. *USA Today.* February 23, 1988.

277. *Human Sexuality,* 2nd ed. William Masters, Virginia Johnson, Robert Kolodny. Little, Brown, and Co. 1985.

278. *1987 Fact Book of US Agriculture.* United States Department of Agriculture.

279. "Distribution of the Adult Female Population in Terms of Specified Body Measurements." Market Research Department, Fairchild Publications, Inc. 1970.

280. "Men's Height/Weight Measurements." Market Research Department, Fairchild Publications, Inc. 1982.

281. Business Week/Harris Poll. March 14, 1988.

282. Quackery—a $10 Billion Scandal. A Report by the Chairman of the Subcommittee on Health and Long-Term Care of the Select Committee on Aging, House of Representatives Ninety-Eighth Congress. 1984.

283. "A Survey of the Status of the American Family, With Special Emphasis on the State of Child-Rearing." Louis Harris and Associates, Inc. Prepared for Philip Morris Companies, Inc. 1987.

284. "Foods Not Eaten by Americans." Anthony Gallo and James Blaylock. *Consumer Research.* Summer 1981.

285. *Society.* November/December 1987.

286. *Society.* January/February 1988.

287. "Food Intakes: Individuals in 48 States, Year 1977–78." Human Nutrition Information Service, US Department of Agriculture. 1983.

288. "Foods Commonly Eaten by Individuals: Amount Per Day and Per Eating Occasion." Human Nutrition Information Service, US Department of Agriculture. 1982.

About the Author
Daniel Evan Weiss is a writer living in New York City.

About the Illustrator
Patrick McDonnell illustrated the Russell Baker column in the *New York Times Magazine*. He is also the author of "Bad Baby" and co-author of *Krazy Kat: The Art of George Herriman*. His cartoons appear regularly in numerous national publications.